LUXURY CHINA

MARKET OPPORTUNITIES AND POTENTIAL

LUXURY CHINA

MARKET OPPORTUNITIES AND POTENTIAL

MICHEL CHEVALIER
AND
PIERRE LU

FOREWORD BY SIDNEY TOLEDANO
PRESIDENT & CEO, CHRISTIAN DIOR COUTURE

WILEY

JOHN WILEY & SONS (ASIA) PTE. LTD.

Published in 2010 by John Wiley & Sons (Asia) Pte. Ltd.
2 Clementi Loop, #02-01, Singapore 129809

Other Wiley Editorial Offices
John Wiley & Sons, Inc., 111 River Street, Hoboken, NJ 07030, USA
John Wiley & Sons, Ltd., The Atrium, Southern Gate, Chichester,
   West Sussex P019 8SQ, UK
John Wiley & Sons (Canada), Ltd., 5353 Dundas Street West, Suite 400,
   Toronto, Ontario M9B 6H8, Canada
John Wiley & Sons Australia Ltd., 42 McDougall Street, Milton, Queensland
   4064, Australia
Wiley-VCH, Boschstrasse 12, D-69469 Weinheim, Germany

Library of Congress Cataloging-in-Publication Data
ISBN: 978-0-470-823415

Printed in Singapore by Saik Wah Press Pte. Ltd.
10 9 8 7 6 5 4 3 2 1

This book is dedicated to our wives,
Sophie and Qian Qian

CONTENTS

W HY A BOOK ABOUT LUXURY IN CHINA? Because China will become in a few years the number one market in the world, given its large population and the growing buying power of the Chinese. It will therefore become a very strong market for top European brands.

China will also become for every luxury business the center of their Asian development. In the future, many products will be developed with a specific Asian target or at least, an Asian interest. This approach will integrate as much as possible the desires of clients in Shanghai, Beijing, and Hong Kong.

The Chinese zone will therefore become more than just an important market for French and Italian brands and will become a priority and, in part, a secondary source of inspiration.

Many new ideas and trends will originate from China. It will become more and more difficult in the future to develop products and brands without taking into account what is happening in Beijing and Shanghai, understanding how women in Hong Kong like to dress or how Taiwanese clients or even Chinese people living abroad view sophistication, fashion, and luxury.

As indicated in this book, it is obvious that China is becóming more than just a luxury market. It will develop into a major source of new brands and new products. In the long run, China will probably become a major supplier of new ideas, new talent and new brands in the luxury field.

This is why Christian Dior considers China as a major market and approaches China from a product side as well as from a creative side. A clear indication of our interest in Chinese creativity is the recent exhibition held by Christian Dior at the Ullens center in Beijing. We asked major Chinese artists, painters, sculptors, photographers and plastic specialists to give their interpretation of the Christian Dior brand using its dresses, its aesthetic values, its 'iconic accessories' and the ambiance of its boutiques as sources of inspiration. We asked the artists to share with us and with the general public what makes Dior a synonym for luxury.

What gives Dior this unique aura is a very special combination of passion for elegance and the never ending quest for contemporary beauty. This quest is a major source of creativity for the House of Dior and China is, without doubt, a source of inspiration and challenges.

The merit of this book, *Luxury China: Market Opportunities and Potential*, is that it is the first one to clearly indicate and to substantiate the fact the China has become a priority for the most dynamic brands and it gives very clear indications about the way in which the market should be developed.

Sidney Toledano
President and CEO
Christian Dior Couture

L UXURY CHINA? Why do we believe there is a need for such a
book? Let us explain what we mean by Luxury China.
A luxury product has to have a strong artistic content. It
must be the result of craftsmanship; and it must be international.
The *raison d'être* of a luxury brand is to be selective and exclusive.
But how exclusive and how selective? For us, Lacoste and Hugo Boss
are luxury goods because they provide sophisticated fashion products
in an environment which generally remains controlled by the brand
owner for sales in self-standing stores, department stores and multi-
brand stores.

Is *luxury* very different from top *fashion*?[1] For some analysts, the
two terms are quite different: a textile and accessories brand, for
example, might start out as a fashion brand and would only be given
the status of a "luxury" brand when it has achieved some stability and
a quality of "timelessness." According to that view, a new fashion
brand has to be creative and come up with new ideas, new concepts
and new products for every season, in order to attract the interest
of the consumers. However, as it develops "classical" models that

sell year in and year out, becoming permanent best-sellers with a signature style, its status will move from fashion to luxury. While this distinction between fashion brand and luxury brand is a valid one, it is also misleading and possibly even dangerous. It is misleading because even if it has achieved "luxury" status, a fashion brand such as Chanel or Dior must still come up with new designs each season, and present them in new ways, in order to retain customers' interest. It is also dangerous because it implies that a luxury brand does not have to innovate to the same extent as a fashion brand, which obviously is not the case.

But at this stage, rather than pursuing this theoretical discussion of the most adequate definition, it may be more productive to describe the different sectors of activity that we will be examining here, as follows:

- The exclusive **Ready-to-Wear** category, for women and men, which includes, of course, all the selective fashion brands such as Chanel, Valentino, Burberry and Versace; the more traditional brands such as Lacoste and Hugo Boss, as indicated above; and also Ports 1981, which is quite selective in its approach to product and distribution, particularly in China.
- The luxury **jewelry and watches** segment is clearly part of this world and is very important in China.
- **Perfumes and cosmetics**, when sold through selective distribution channels, are clearly luxury products, even if they correspond to low-priced items.
- **Fashion accessories** brands are run as sister brands of fashion brands. This category includes handbags and leather goods, and also shoes, belts and any other element of a woman's total "look", such as glasses, writing instruments, lighters and so on. For men, it also includes ties and shirts and other elements of their wardrobe.
- **Wines and spirits** are the only examples of luxury products available in supermarkets and food outlets. But the product concept and positioning of wines and spirits require a level of sophistication that sets these products apart and makes them an important part of the luxury sector.

- While **luxury automobiles, luxury tourism and private banking** are also clearly part of this luxury category, we will not address them directly in this book because they require very different distribution strategies.

In this book, our definition of "China" is, for the most part, restricted to the mainland, which requires quite different distribution and promotional tools from those used in, say, Hong Kong, Macau or even Taiwan.

But why address the topic of luxury in mainland China at all? The answer is simple enough: in the last decade China has become a very major economic power, with an annual growth rate in the region of 10% and, allowing for differences in Purchasing Price Parity, will soon surpass the United States in the volume of products it manufactures and services it delivers.

For luxury goods, China has certainly become a very important market, as we discuss at length in Chapter 1. As Bernard Arnault said in November 2005: "We knew [China] would someday be the biggest market in the world. Whether it would be in 20, 30, 40 years, it was irreversible."[2]

So, in what sense is this a challenge? China is a very difficult market. It is the most populous nation in the world, with 57 cities of more than one million inhabitants. Where do you start and how do you deal with such a powerful and diversified country when you want to begin distribution operations here? As we will see in chapters 2 and 3, while Chinese consumers are very interested in luxury products and major luxury brands, it takes time and money to convince them that they should buy a given brand rather than another.

Is it easy to be profitable in China? If large brands have a relatively easy time of it,[3] medium brands undoubtedly find it more difficult to build the necessary volume to offset the minimum costs of operation and of advertising and promotional investments. And smaller brands face the difficult challenge of investing in brand communication and awareness to be able to gain a foothold in this huge market. But profitability is only one part of the issue. Given the very impressive growth of the luxury market in China, a brand must invest heavily in new stores, new inventories and new accounts receivables to keep pace; and even for profitable brands, major cash injections are often required to increase their local investments.

But the challenge is not merely financial and economic. Developing Chinese activities requires a strong understanding of the way business is conducted and of the basic cultural values and reactions of 1.4 billion inhabitants.

Our regular contact with foreign brands operating in China and with Chinese brands planning to expand their operations worldwide has prompted us to describe in depth this very specific market and to give indications of the best ways to operate. The opportunities on offer in this rapidly expanding market are such that it deserves very special attention and very special investment.

We believe this book will be useful both for executives already operating in China or for those looking at opportunities to start activities here. But it is also addressed to all analysts, journalists and scholars who are interested in luxury brands in general and in the Chinese market in particular.

The objective of this book is to give a better understanding of the Chinese luxury market. We provide a general analysis of the Chinese market and its potential, and describe what we consider the key to successful operations in China. The first chapter deals with the market size. This has not been an easy chapter to write because in this huge country, information is sparse and difficult to obtain. But we wanted to give an idea of the market potential and see if the economists and journalists who are presenting China as the second luxury market in the world, behind Japan, are right.

The second and third chapters describe the Chinese consumers. In Chapter 2, we have gathered all existing information about customer spending power and purchasing behavior. We have shown who is buying luxury goods and to what extent each customer group develops purchase patterns. We have focused particularly on the up-and-coming middle class which, in China like in every country in the world, is the primary source of business potential for the luxury market. In Chapter 3, we have focused on the attitudes of Chinese customers toward luxury and on how the purchase of expensive luxury items fits with traditional Chinese culture and accepted standards of behavior.

In Chapter 4, we explain the different ways to enter the Chinese market, be it through a subsidiary or, at the beginning at least, through a distributor. In a market which is changing very fast and which is very new to the luxury business, we felt it was necessary to explain who the major distributors and professionals of the market are. Chapter 5, outlines the considerations for retailing and licensing in China.

In Chapter 6, we examine what makes China different from other countries and concentrate on the specific communication tools that are the most effective there. In the last chapter, we speak about brand and design registration systems in China, of brand protection and of the best ways to curb counterfeit activities which remain an important area of concern for major brands.

At the end of each chapter, we present a business case of luxury brands operating in China. The aim here is to show different approaches to the Chinese market and to communicate how the diversity of situations and market positions fit into that complex luxury market. The case studies have all been written from outside sources and with no specific arrangements or agreements with the brands concerned. In each case, we describe the brand's major achievements to date and discuss the specific business challenges and opportunities.

One of these case studies deals with Louis Vuitton, which is probably the leading luxury brand in China. We describe its positioning and its retail strength and the way it has learnt, over time, to deal with the Chinese consumer. But if there is a lot to learn from big success stories, it is also important to describe cases of brands that are not so successful at the worldwide level and this is why the Alfred Dunhill case finds its place here. A masculine brand, which has done well in the United Kingdom and in Japan, it started very early in China, and is moving up rapidly. The issue here is what it should do next and how this may change the company focus at the worldwide level.

We have also decided to present Chinese brand cases, because we believe China will, in the long term, be a major source of luxury brands. The first of these studies concerns Shiatzy Chen, a brand originating from Taiwan, which has worldwide potential, provided it can develop strongly in mainland China and is able to adjust its product offerings to the needs of an international market. Liuli Gongfang, which might be described as the Chinese equivalent of Daum, is another case in the same category. Also originating from Taiwan, it is very strong in mainland China.

Three other cases offer a mix of Chinese and worldwide activities. In "The War of the Spirits," we look at the competition between major foreign alcohol brands and local traditional Chinese products. The Rolex case study examines the brand's position in a market where Omega has established an extremely strong success story. Shanghai Tang is a brand created by a Hong Kong Chinese businessman, with a Shanghai label, belonging to the Richemont group, and managed from Shanghai by a French executive. This brand conveys a strong Chinese image, but one which is somehow internationalized and geared almost exclusively to foreign customers through establishing a very upscale European style, while maintaining a strong Chinese outlook.

In the appendices, we provide details of all the major cities, with special profiles of Beijing and Shanghai. There are details, too, of magazine audiences, of television channel ratings, of city sizes, that are necessary to operate in China and which we hope may become an indispensable handbook for the Chinese luxury executive.

If this book convinces the reader of the real opportunities of the Chinese market for luxury brands and conveys the diversity of winning marketing strategies to establish a brand in China, we would have met our objectives.

What is certain is that a luxury brand which is absent from, or has only a weak presence in, the Chinese market in 2015 or 2020 will simply no longer have claims to being a worldwide brand.

ENDNOTES

1   For this discussion, see Michel Chevalier and Gérald Mazzalovo's *Luxury Brand Management: A World of Privilege*, John Wiley & Sons, 2008.

2   Quoted in Thomas (2007): 306.

3   Christopher Zanardi Landi, the CEO of Louis Vuitton in China, has been quoted as saying that the company has "never lost any money in any store in China" (see Thomas, op. cit.: 306.)

CHAPTER 1

Challenges and Market Size

To **UNDERSTAND** the challenges of luxury activities in China, one must look at the total size of the business worldwide and then, for each sector of activity, analyze the size of the Chinese market.

While many economists believe that China is the third-largest luxury market in the world, after the United States and Japan, the situation for individual brands is quite different. For example, for Italian fashion brands, Italy remains the primary market, with Japan in second place and the United States in third. When China develops, it will become fourth or fifth. For French fashion brands (with a few exceptions such as Louis Vuitton) the French market remains number one, with China often in fourth or fifth place—which is already quite a performance. For the industry as a whole, Korea is also very strong and profitable, as soon as a critical mass is reached, constituting the fourth-largest market for many brands.

A 2006 study by IPSOS, Paris found that the Chinese market is the fourth-largest in the world behind Japan (40%), the United States (20%) and Europe (17%). Of course, the figures need to be treated with some caution because they appear to be related to the ready-to-wear area rather than considering the luxury market as a whole. Nevertheless, they do give an indication of China's importance in the field.

In global terms, Chinese economists used to include the figures for Hong Kong, Macau and Taiwan in their analyses. These three markets have been developing now for almost 30 years and have reached very high volumes and a high degree of sophistication. Hong Kong's duty-free status enables it to benefit from a large number of tourist purchases, particularly from Japanese and American nationals. Taiwan, while not a duty-free territory, has limited duties and also constitutes another large market of luxury products sold to domestic customers and tourists.

So, when these three territories are included, China is the third- or fourth-largest luxury market in the world. However, it is also important to note the incredible growth that luxury products are experiencing in mainland China.

Also, one should add to such figures the market potential presented by Chinese tourists purchasing luxury products abroad. In 2006, some 35 million mainland Chinese traveled abroad and it is estimated that this figure will reach 100 million by 2015.

To understand the situation one has to start with an evolution of the general worldwide market before studying the specific market situation in China.

The size of the global market

A recent study places the value of the worldwide luxury market at close to US$265 billion at wholesale or corporate value.[1] A breakdown by category is shown in Table 1.1.

TABLE 1.1: *Value of worldwide luxury market by category, 2008 (US$)*

Ready-to-wear	30 billion
Leather goods and accessories	24 billion
Fragrances and cosmetics	41 billion
Spirits, champagnes and still wines	107 billion
Watches	16 billion
Jewelry	40 billion
Others (including Tableware)	7 billion
Total	265 billion

The size of the Chinese mainland market

A breakdown of our estimates of the figures for the Chinese mainland market is given in Table 1.2. The estimated amount of US$15 billion, representing 5.5% of the worldwide market, is very much in line with the figure of US$6 billion produced by the investment

TABLE 1.2: *Value of luxury market in mainland China by category, 2008 (US$)*

Ready-to-wear	1.5 billion
Leather goods and accessories	1.6 billion
Fragrances and cosmetics	4 billion
Spirits, champagnes and still wines	4 billion
Watches	1.3 billion
Jewelry	1.3 billion
Others (including Tableware)	1.3 billion
Total	15 billion

bank Goldman Sachs for 2004, taking into account the present growth rate of luxury goods in China, which, for all luxury categories, can reach 25% a year.

If the figures for Hong Kong, Macau and Taiwan were included, the total for 2008 would probably amount to US$27 billion, or 10% of the worldwide market, but this figure would be skewed by double counting (many products sold in mainland China are imported through Hong Kong and may have been registered at export prices in Hong Kong and then at wholesale or retail prices on the mainland).

While we have mentioned an estimated average yearly growth rate of 25%, the actual figure is very difficult to come by because it depends very much on the sub-categories of luxury products that we may consider.

What is known for sure, however, is that many "iconic" brands were growing at around 30% in their existing stores and were expanding the number of stores by about 20% each year between 2001 and 2007. Together, they provided an additional annual sales growth of 50%. If they wanted to maintain their market position, and if they compare themselves to Prada, Louis Vuitton, or Gucci, they had to invest and keep growing at this rate.

Even if the current growth rate decreases, mainland China's share of the luxury market will reach 15% in 2015. Add in Hong Kong, Macau and Taiwan and it will account for between 20% and 25% of worldwide sales. In categories like fashion and accessories, China and Japan (with approximately 20% of the world's population) between them will represent 50% of the worldwide volume—a clear indication that what happens in these two countries is essential in this business field.

For the past five years, China has, along with Russia, been the fastest-growing market in the world. But whether it is profitable is another issue, and one we will discuss later in this chapter.

The outlook for different market segments

The analysis must now go one step further and look at each product category.

Fashion and accessories

Our estimates for fashion and accessories are still limited, as we are talking of a total of only US$2.6 billion. This market has probably been growing from anywhere between 20% and 30% a year and is very much an "El Dorado" for the very top brands.

This is also the only market in the world where ready-to-wear products for men sell more than ladies' wear. This is of course due to the very keen interest in luxury products among men, and the fact that men control their own budgets, while only women with an active business life have clear financial autonomy.

Brands such as Louis Vuitton, Chanel, Gucci and Salvatore Ferragamo have different profiles. Louis Vuitton has 21 stores, Chanel three stores, Gucci 17 stores, and Salvatore Ferragamo 23 stores. Other brands which are perhaps not very well-known in Europe (the Canadian brand Ports 1961, for example) are developing very rapidly.

In fashion, the merchandise sold in the various stores is very dependent on the profiles of their clientele. In China, men are buying more often than women. This is why in the merchandise mix, accessories form the majority of sales, and in ladies' fashion, simple tops are purchased more often than sophisticated dresses.

However, as men may buy fashion goods from the same brand from the same store at the same time for their *tai tais* (wives) and for their *er tais* ("second wives"/girlfriends)—a traditional style for one and a flashier look for the other—there is a need for very diversified merchandise.

The fact that men are important customers for luxury products to an extent that is rare in other countries provides an additional opportunity for men's lines. The clearest case of this is Ermenegildo Zegna, whose 52 Chinese stores (including franchises) make China one of its most important markets.

Another problem for luxury fashion products in China is that the large price difference between, for example, a branded luxury jacket and a jacket purchased for a few dollars in an open-air market is huge. There is a need for basic training so that the consumer can understand the difference and feel confident about such products. In some cases, for example, the consumers don't want to buy a dress simply because they are afraid of giving it to their local dry-cleaner with a pile of standard dresses.

In the ready-to-wear category, Chinese men (like their Japanese counterparts) like basic colors for their suits, and have a strong preference for white or light-blue shirts. Women are slightly more modern in their taste. They like to use strong colors and have a very strong taste for pant suits over skirt suits.

In the fashion sector, the major brands have no difficulty finding an acceptable balance between growth and cash. Smaller brands, on the other hand, don't find it very easy to develop. If they want to operate their own stores, they must have a presence in Shanghai, Beijing and Guangzhou at least. If they want to be known by Chinese customers, they have to advertise and organize public relations activities and, perhaps, special fashion shows without any guarantee that this will produce an immediate increase in sales.

Fendi's solution to this problem was to organize an event that would both raise its profile in China and be large enough to be seen and mentioned around the world. The fashion show it organized on the Great Wall in December 2007 certainly had a great impact in Europe, the United States, and Asia.

Department stores provide another avenue of operation, although the set-up is perhaps not ideal for top-range luxury brands. So many brands have flagship stores in Hong Kong or multi-brand store activities and are still considering whether it is worthwhile setting up on the mainland. Distributors such as Bluebell, which had developed activities for fashion brands in China, pulled out once they realized that it would take them a very long time to make any money. Uncertainty continues over whether their "principals" would be willing to sign distribution agreements that could start with a prolonged period of losses and without any guarantee of long-term profitability.

What is striking in China is that many medium-size international fashion brands have a very limited visibility or are absent altogether. Rather than finding diversity, one is confronted with a few very large brands, trying to be as powerful as possible. In the long run, this may be a problem because it is its diversity, its difference and its creativity that makes fashion interesting.

Wines and spirits

The wines and spirits market in China is not easy to assess as it includes three different product categories. The first of these comprises imported spirits and includes, for example, Hennessy Cognac and Johnnie Walker whisky which are sold though the Diageo-LVMH joint venture and have a strong presence in the clubs and bars. It also includes Pernod Ricard's Chivas and Royal Salute whiskies and Martell cognac. Rémy Cointreau also has a strong presence with Rémy Martin, which for a long time was the number-one cognac in China, but has had to give way to Hennessy, which has invested heavily to promote its product in conjunction with bars and nightclubs.

In this category, too, we must include other foreign companies such as Bacardi or Brown Forman and all their brands, which are also sold in restaurants and nightclubs as well as supermarkets or expensive food-and-liquor stores.

The second category includes wines that have been developed locally in the territory. In 2006, China consumed 495 million liters of wine or around 650 million bottles. This represented sales of approximately US$1.7 billion. This was predicted to increase to the point where, by 2012, China will be the eighth-biggest wine consumer in the world.

According to Channel Consulting Ltd in Beijing, dry red wines represent 68% of the consumption, sweet red wines 23%, and dry white wine 8%. It is estimated that 65% of wine is purchased in supermarkets, 25% in hotels, restaurants and clubs, 9% in bars and 1% in specialist stores.[2]

Most of the consumption is of domestic wines. In this very large market, three brands represent half of the total: Changyu (a local brand created in 1914), Dynasty (created by Rémy Cointreau in 1980) and Great Wall (a local initiative started in 1985). Imports represent only 15%, with more than 10% of this coming from bulk wines, mainly from France (40%) and branded in China, often with Chinese names and a Chinese presentation, as is the case for Imperial Court.

A third category comprises domestic spirits, including white liquor (generally made of grains or potatoes and containing over 40% alcohol). The leader in this market is Maotai from the Maotai group.

It also includes "yellow liquor," which is generally brewed from sticky rice and contains between 15% and 18% alcohol.

The final category of Chinese "spirits" is beer, but this product certainly does not belong to the luxury market.

Overall, the market has traditionally been growing at approximately 30% a year.

Watches

Watches are very important in China as they are a product selected by men. It is estimated that 75% of watches purchased are bought as gifts, and generally business gifts. A common arrangement is for men to select the watch they want and for it to be paid for by a business associate. This market, which represents 10% of worldwide sales, is worth about US$1.3 billion, with an annual growth rate of 20%. This includes products entering from Hong Kong, and licensed watches from the likes of Charles Jourdan, Sonia Rykiel and Bertolucci which are made in China, as well as combination watches that are manufactured and sold locally.

The Chinese luxury-watch market seems to be concentrated in middle-range luxury products. Omega alone commands approximately 30% of the market and is followed by Rolex, Longines, Rado and Tissot.

Perfumes and cosmetics

Unlike their Japanese counterparts, Chinese consumers are interested in fragrances, skin care and make-up. Import statistics for 2006 give a figure of US$300 million; again, though, a lot of products are manufactured locally under the Dior or Estée Lauder brands, for example.

Before a product can be sold in China, it should be officially registered with the Chinese authorities. This is of course a long process, and it is also quite expensive; which means that before the importer can recoup the registration costs, it must sell a large number of products and be able to sell to many individual stores.

But statistics for Chinese products tell a different story. For 2006 the cosmetics industry reported national sales of US$14 billion, as follows:

Skin care	40%	US$5.6 billion
Beauty care (including make-up)	15%	US$2.1 billion
Hairdressing care and perfumery	40%	US$5.6 billion
Others	5%	US$0.7 billion

The difficulty here, of course, is to distinguish between mass-market and selective products. A large part of the hairdressing care and perfumery category, for example, comes from shampoos, which are very far from being luxury items.

There are some 300 cosmetics brands found in China, 80% of which are foreign brands. The market is expected to grow between 10% and 20% per year for the next five years.

Customs statistics show an export value for 2006 of US$812 million, much of which relates to international branded products partly manufactured in China and sold elsewhere in the world.

International brands are also acquiring Chinese domestic brands. In 2004, for example, L'Oréal purchased the YUE SAI cosmetic brand, named after a very successful Chinese celebrity businesswoman in Shanghai.

The strength of the foreign brands remains very clear: for selective make-up products, for example, 16 of the top 20 international brands are officially operating in China and overseas brands occupy the top 10 places in market share.[3]

The consumers of perfumes and cosmetics fall into three groups, which require different approaches:

- very wealthy women: 1% of the urban population
- the middle-aged, medium-income group: 2.5% of the urban population
- the rural market: 50% of the rural population.

For selective products, the market is limited to the first two categories and to 3.5% of the city population, or approximately 20 million inhabitants with a relatively high standard of living.

Consumers are generally quite young. Women from 18 to 24 years old are the first generation to use make-up. They like colorful products with a preference for eye products. In the 25–30 age group, skin care is the leading product category. The over-35s are still quite difficult to convince and many remain non-users of selective products.[4] In the north of the country, consumers prefer very strong colors, while in the south they are more conservative.[5] Chinese women are still in the process of discovering new products, new brands and new uses, which explains why products are bought either on impulse or to be given to friends. Gifts are a very important way for young consumers to get acquainted with these particular products.

For perfumes, consumers are looking for light flagrances (fruity or light floral). They are still relatively price conscious and priority is given to smaller sizes (30 ml sprays, for example).

For skin care, whitening products is the largest category, followed by anti-wrinkle products. In make-up, lipsticks lead the way, followed by mascara.

The country of origin of these products is similar to the situation worldwide, as summarized in Tables 1.3 and 1.4.

For selective products, Lancôme is doing extremely well, with 20% of the market. Shiseido, which has been in China for a long time, is also quite strong, and constitutes a large part of the Japanese imports shown in Table 1.4. Christian Dior is also quite strong, building very much on its early entry with two brands: Christian Dior, of course, and a lower-priced second brand, Mademoiselle de Paris, which has since been phased out.

TABLE 1.3: *Imports of perfumes by country of origin, 2006*

France	59.6%
U.S.A.	25.3%
U.K.	5.9%
Spain	4.2%
Italy	2.7%
Germany	1.2%
Others	1.1%
Total	100.0%

Source: *"Le marché du luxe en Chine et à Hong Kong,"* March 2007, UBIFRANCE

TABLE 1.4: *Imports of cosmetics by country of origin, 2006*

France	33.3%
U.S.A.	20.5%
Japan	20.4%
South Korea	6.2%
U.K.	3.5%
Italy	3.5%
Others	12.6%
Total	100.0%

Source: *"Le marché du luxe en Chine et à Hong Kong,"* March 2007, UBIFRANCE

Jewelry

The very high estimate of jewelry sales in Table 1.2 reflects the Chinese consumer's liking for gold. Each year, China consumes 253 tons of gold, making it the third-largest gold market in the world, with 8% of world consumption.

The largest part of this market, however, is very traditional, with most products sold unbranded. Also, the importance of men in the purchasing of branded goods works against the sales of sophisticated feminine jewelry. In a way, the mix of watches and jewelry in China is very much to the advantage of watches.

Another distinguishing characteristic of the Chinese market is that rings represent 75% of total jewelry sales, well ahead of bracelets, necklaces, earrings or brooches. As could be expected, men's jewelry pieces account for a very small part (perhaps only 5%) of the total.

Basically, a very large part of jewelry pieces sold in China are Chinese-made and even brands like HIERSUN (with six stores in Shanghai, Beijing, Harbin and Tianjin with an average size of 1,500 square meters) or FANGHUA (with six stores—two in Beijing and four in Shanghai—of up to 1,000 square meters) are developing rapidly, along with international brands like Cartier, Bulgari or Tiffany (eight stores). The Chinese jewelry market is extremely dynamic and branded products will play an increasingly important role in the near future.

TABLE 1.5: *Imports of jewelry by country of origin, 2006*

Switzerland	24.6%
Hong Kong	20.2%
France	10.1%
South Korea	9.1%
Japan	7.5%
Italy	6.8%
South Africa	4.9%
Others	16.8%
Total	100.0%

Source: "Le marché du luxe en Chine et à Hong Kong," March 2007, UBIFRANCE

Accessible vs. top luxury

Given that the Chinese market is new and developing rapidly, it may be tempting to consider it as a top-end market, with wealthy individuals contributing a large part to luxury sales. These individuals buy expensive "iconic" products and price is not really an issue. The fact that prices are arrived at on an international basis and are not based on local standards of living does not seem to be a major consideration.

But, as in any developing market, part of the impressive growth rate comes from the fact that the new middle class are also becoming luxury customers. Many women now carry a Louis Vuitton bag or wear Salvatore Ferragamo shoes. These purchases are still a major investment for them, given their monthly salary, but they will do it to feel cosmopolitan, modern and sexy.

Can we then say that there is no price elasticity in China? Actually, for many products such as wine or make-up, price is a very important part of the final purchase decision. But for a luxury watch, this is not really the case.

Is China a profitable market?

Major brands are investing heavily to take advantage of China's growth and are profitable. Brands belonging to the second tier have more difficulty: they still have a limited awareness and must invest to improve this. They continue to experience difficulties in opening profitable luxury stores on their own and are still losing money. They know they must invest much more, simply to exist and to keep their market position.

So the answer to the profitability question is, in cash terms, a clear "no." As brands open new stores, and they must do so at a rate of 20% every year just to keep pace with the market, they have to invest in new leases, new inventories, new decor and the hiring and training of new personnel. Also, the opening of each store requires heavy promotion before it can reach a significant customer base, so there is a necessity to invest heavily and to bring cash from other operations to sustain this growth rate.

In profit-and-loss terms, the picture is not much rosier. At this stage, brands must develop their consumer awareness among a growing number of customers, and they must therefore invest in advertising and promotion at a higher level than what is considered the worldwide norm in their product categories.

Some brands estimate that their level of sales per square meter is three-times lower in mainland China than it is in Japan. Of course, in China the cost of sales staff is much lower, but it all boils down to the rental cost of a store in a top location in Shanghai, Beijing or Guangzhou. And today, Chinese rental rates are quite expensive.

It is sometimes rumored that in large luxury shopping malls, real-estate owners are ready to reduce, or even forget about, the rent to attract top luxury brands. They believe that by giving free space to major brands they will ensure that their centers are attractive to consumers. In a way, it is as if the struggling "middle brands" are being asked to pay for the top luxury brands, something only those that have been in China for quite some time (such as Kenzo or Givenchy) can afford to do.

In a way, being strong in mainland China is an expensive proposition. Large brands are happy to make the necessary investment, given the worldwide growth it provides. Smaller brands have difficulty keeping up with the pace and investing heavily in still-unprofitable activities, when their total worldwide business itself is not so profitable. In the long run, however, the market will mature and a larger number of brands will be recognized and appreciated; but this will take time.

Is there room, then, for very small brands and can they survive through sales in department stores or in multi-brand stores? We will analyze this point later. For the moment, though, suffice to say that developing in China is not a simple venture. Prices become an issue when the imported international brand is compared to those of its local competitors. Advertising becomes vital to lift the brand above the crowd, and to promote the imported brand as a strong alternative to locally made brands.

In a way the Chinese luxury market is an El Dorado for strong brands but it can be a nightmare for small ones. What is certain is that, handled effectively and with high priority, the Chinese market can provide growth, visibility and, also, sales outside of China as Chinese tourists increasingly travel abroad.

But some industry executives complain about the difficulty of making money in China and Eric Douilhet, the president of Bluebell, has been quoted even before the economic crisis as saying that "People are too optimistic about China."[6] How accurate an assessment is this? Are the brands that are strong in China today profitable? Ivan Kwok, of the Boston Consulting Group, says: "If you are not the number one brand, if you are number two or three, the odds are good your fingers will be burned . . . China is a growing force in the luxury business, but the market is not large enough yet to accommodate so many players. Only about one in 10 overseas consumer-goods companies are profitable in China."[7]

Even if rents and staff are cheaper than, say, in Japan, the need to develop brand awareness in a very large market is quite costly. Import duties and value-added taxes mean that companies are charging higher prices in China than, say, in a duty-free city like Hong Kong. Retail prices for ready-to-wear or leather accessories can be 35% higher in mainland China than in Hong Kong.

So it is not right to say that Chinese customers become purchasers of luxury goods as soon as they reach a certain level of income. The process is a little more complicated than that. When consumers have an income below a certain level, say US$40,000 a year, they are not luxury-goods customers. Even when their income exceeds this, if they have never traveled abroad and are not aware of luxury brands, they may not be interested in those products. It is only when their income exceeds US$40,000 and they or their families have the opportunity to travel and become acquainted with luxury brands, that they become regular customers. When they do travel abroad or make regular trips to Hong Kong, it is there that they make a considerable percentage of their luxury purchases.

The fact that China recently decided to put a special luxury tax on the purchase of expensive watches has not helped the situation. It is certainly not the case that consumers are rushing to the luxury stores, and there is still a great deal to do to create the necessary relationship between luxury brands and the Chinese public.

The fact that many brands are not yet profitable in China is only one part of the story. Some brands have too limited a presence: they need to advertise nationally to improve their brand awareness and they don't have sufficient stores to harvest the impact of their investment. The views of Nigel Luk, Cartier General Manager for China, are very much in line with this: "If you are looking for quick profits, don't go to China: it takes a long time to be profitable," he said, pointing out that although Cartier then had 14 boutiques on the mainland it would likely be another 15 years before it met its profit target.[8] This would certainly require many more stores and major additional investments.

The paradox of the situation is that the only way major brands can attain profitability and keep their competitive standing is to open new stores; to establish sufficient presence on the market; to keep up with the strong growth of the market; and take maximum advantage of the opportunities.

There is no doubt that the Chinese market is an important one and growing very fast. The market is quite open and everybody is welcome. However, it would be a big mistake to think that business can be financed simply from returns on investments made from start-up operations.

The impact of the financial crisis

The ongoing financial crisis that beset the world economy in 2008 will dent anticipated growth rates in China's luxury business by 20% to 50%. However, the potential for the luxury industry remains significant; but it will require more sophisticated business plans from the luxury firms for it to be realized.

China's economic outlook

China's GDP growth for 2008 will be 9.6% and is forecast to reach between 5% and 7% in 2009. However, these figures are being questioned by foreign observers, who say that because the Chinese economy is fueled by its export activities, it will not be able to grow its domestic economy during a worldwide crisis. While they are right in this, they forget that these export activities represent only 35% of the Chinese GDP.

To continue to grow in these difficult times, the Chinese economy is redirecting its focus to the domestic market. President Hu Jintao clearly indicated that he will put major emphasis on the development of the economy through basic investments rather than private consumption. He has said the economy will be given full priority and in December 2008 he indicated that he was ready to inject US$500 billion to develop it. He also spoke of gradual reforms and a new drive for major infrastructure projects.

November 2008 provided a good indication of what may well happen in 2009. Although exports were still growing by 19% in October 2008 compared to October 2007, the November figure was 2% lower than the November 2007 dollar volume. But imports for November 2008 compared to November 2007 had dropped even more, resulting in an exceptional trade surplus of US$40 billion. This reduction in exports, coupled with an even greater reduction in imports, will be the picture for some time to come.

Stories of Chinese factories being closed down, with business relocated elsewhere, often appear on TV news programs. Part of this is due to a very poorly timed labor law, which became effective in January 2008. In Guangdong province, for example, some Hong Kong businesses are relocating plants to Vietnam. But even if this can be considered a marginal trend and one which the Chinese authorities are working hard to prevent, it may have affected several thousand factories and some experts say that up to 20 million workers have been laid off. However, even if growth for 2009 falls to around 6%, it will probably return to a higher rate in 2010.

Spending patterns

When individuals find that their assets are depreciating—through a decline in the property or stock markets, for example—they become more careful about their purchases, even though their income might remain undiminished.

Reduced individual consumption leads to major changes in consumer spending patterns. For example, ACNielsen has fore-cast a drop of 15% in gambling revenues for the Macau Casino for 2009. This will obviously have a concomitant effect on shopping in Macau. Here again, the Chinese authorities have got the timing very wrong: in trying to cut tax evasion, they increased the restric-tions on Chinese citizens wishing to travel to Macau, from once a month to once every three months. This has had a strong impact on gambling and commercial activities.

The automobile market is another case in point. The market was growing by 20% until June 2008, but sales fell at approximately the same rate in the final six months of the year.

The impact on luxury activities

The effect of all this on the luxury business will differ according to category. Small-ticket items such as perfumes and cosmetics and wines and spirits will, as usual, be less affected, as these prod-ucts are considered countercyclical, with sales leveling off in 2009 before growing again in 2010 and returning to high growth in 2011. Fashion and ready-to-wear, which was very much affected in 2008, will have difficulties in 2009 and will recuperate afterwards.

Expensive products such as watches or high-priced fashion items, which are generally the most affected by a crisis, will have a difficult time but will probably get back to 15% growth rates in the future.

Overall, we can expect the Chinese luxury business to grow by 10–15% in 2009 and to get back to 20% in 2010. However, brands will be affected differently by this. Strong brands will continue to develop and grow much faster than the market, while weaker brands will have major difficulties in keeping up, even with the reduced growth of the market.

Here again, major brands such as Hermès, which are viewed by consumers as secure and fall-back investments, will be the least affected by the situation.

ENDNOTES

1 See Chevalier and Mazzalovo, 2008: 22. Note that this does not take into account the figures done in their stores by independent retailers who have purchased luxury products at wholesale prices.

2 Vertumne International & Associés, "The Chinese wine market: Opportunities and Threats."

3 *Cosmetic News China*, September 2007, overseas issue No.46: 1.

4 "Le marché du Luxe en Chine et à Hong Kong," March 2007, UBIFRANCE.

5 *Management Review*, Paris, January 2009.

6 "Luxury products struggle for profit in China," Le Hin Lim, *International Herald Tribune*, February 1, 2007. Based on a speech at the Hong Kong Chamber of Commerce in October 2006.

7 Ibid.

8 Ibid.

Alfred Dunhill[1]

Company history

Since 1893, when Alfred Dunhill took over his father's saddlery business in London, the company has established itself worldwide as a leading purveyor of men's luxury items ranging from leather goods and motoring accessories to watches and writing instruments; from tobacco products to menswear and fragrances. From the beginning, dunhill products were never necessities but, rather, objects of privilege. By the mid 1960s, dunhill stores could be found in 100 countries, including Hong Kong and Japan. Its first menswear line was created for sale in the Asian markets, and menswear has continued to fare well in the Asia-Pacific region. In 1997, Richemont became the company's primary shareholder.

Products

Since its beginnings, dunhill has provided its customers with a variety of distinguished products: from menswear to writing instruments, leather goods, jewelry, timepieces, gifts, and games. Its distinguishing factor lies in its ability to select raw materials from the world's leading tanneries, molding them into elegantly crafted, handmade briefcases, luggage and so on.

A sampling of products and prices found in dunhill's collections—which are designed to evoke all the characteristics expected of a private-members' club—include a traditional attaché case which retails for US$4,015, silk ties for US$130, billfolds averaging US$250, hand-stitched lamb Nappa driving gloves for US$250, and a Camdeboo mohair blazer that can be purchased for US$1,795. Rollagas lighters range from US$440 to US$13,000. Pens can also range from US$255 to US$1,195. Dunhill watches range from US$2,425 to US$6,200 for the Facet 1936, for example.

Dunhill Homes

A recent "product" development for dunhill has been its construction of global "homes." Dunhill "homes" are stores situated in beautifully nostalgic mansions in London, Shanghai, and in a prime street-front Ginza address in Tokyo. Each multi-purpose "home" carries an exquisite array of carefully selected products. In London, for example, Bourdon House (opened in August 2008 in the former London residence of the Duke of Westminster) has rooms for gadgets, menswear, accessories and custom-made clothing. The message is clear: no other place fully dedicates its space to the careful upkeep of men. In addition, Bourdon House offers limited-edition products and vintage "museum" pieces, spa treatment rooms, a traditional gentleman's Barber, a private screening room, and the Cellar Bar.

In Tokyo, dunhill's first "home" resides in the city's luxury shopping district of Ginza. The Tokyo home's façade was designed by leading architectural designer Tatsuya Matsui. Complementing the menswear and leather-goods collections are specific pieces sourced directly from London's top vintage luxury goods purveyor, Bentley's. Similar to the London home, the Tokyo home offers grooming services at The Barber—serviced by Ginza Matsunaga, famed for its use of advanced grooming techniques—and houses a lounge, The Aquarium, and the Valet—a professional wardrobe-maintenance team of multiple clothing-care specialists.

Shanghai's dunhill Home is found in a perfectly restored 1920s neoclassical villa in the former French Concession, tucked away off the busy Huai Hai Road shopping area. With the committed goal "to advance the pursuit of male indulgence," Shanghai's home successfully recreates the opulence of Shanghai's decadent past. Like both London and Tokyo homes, Huai Hai Road 796 has a Travel & Discovery Room, with pieces from dunhill's archives, a Bespoke Tailoring Room (which also offers custom-made leather), the White Shirt Bar, and a Barber. A feature exclusive to Shanghai is the fine-dining, members-only restaurant, KEE, and the leading contemporary Chinese art gallery ShanghART.

Alfred Dunhill's Home in Shanghai (left, ground and second floors). The Kee Club is on the third and fourth floors. Vacheron Constantin's flagship store is on the right.
Copyright: Alfred Dunhill

Business development in China

In the 1960s Alfred Dunhill began to develop business in Asia by opening stores in Hong Kong and Japan. Later, the company expanded into Taiwan, Singapore, and Malaysia, but it wasn't until 1994 that dunhill entered mainland China, where it now operates 42 stores as well as overseeing nearly 40 franchised retail stores (see Figure 1).

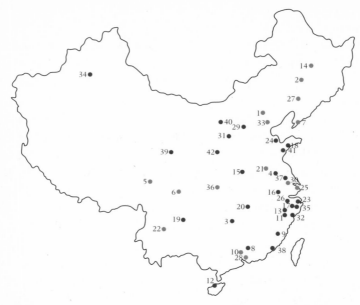

1. Beijing
   - CCP
   - China World
     Hotel
   - Sogo Dept. Store
   - Scitech Plaza
   - Lufthansa Ctr.
   - Oriental Plaza
   - Parkson Dept. Store
   - Shuang An
   - Seasons Place
     Shopping Ctr.
   - Beijing Airport
   - Lufthansa Outlet
   - Jinyuan Temp
2. Changchun
   - Charter Times
     Square
3. Changsha
   - Dolton Hotel
   - Brilliance Orient
     Plaza
4. Changzhou
   - Time Fortune Plaza
5. Chengdu
   - Ren He Zong Bei
     Dept. Store
   - Ren He Ren Dong
6. Chongqing
   - Metropolitan Plaza
   - Maison Mode
   - Airport
7. Dalian
   - Mykal
     Corporation
   - Wharf Time Square

8. Foshan
   - Sunlink
9. Fuzhou
   - Orient Dept. Store
10. Guangzhou
    - (10-1) Friendship
      Dept. Store
11. Guiyang
    - Zhi Cheng
      Avenue
    - Lavant Dept. Store
12. Hainan
    - Sang Sang Dept. Store
13. Handan
    - International
      Trade
14. Harbin
    - New World Dept. Store
    - Mykal
15. Hefei
    - Vista
16. Huzhou
    - Zhebei
17. Jiangyin
    - Hualian
18. Jinan
    - Gui He Dept. Store
19. Kunming
    - Golden Dragon
      Dept. Store
    - Gingko Dept. Store
20. Nanchang
    - Parkson Dept. Store

21. Nanjing
    - Deji
    - Golden Eagle
      Dept. Store
22. Nanning
    - Dreams Island
      Dept. Store
23. Ningbo
    - New World Dept. Store
    - Tian Yi Square
24. Qingdao
    - Printemps Plaza
    - Sunshine
25. Shanghai
    - Plaza 66
    - Oriental Shopping Ctr.
    - Sogo Dept. Store
    - Friendship Store
    - Yaohan Dept. Store
    - SH Home
    - Qingpu
26. Shangyu
    - Datong
27. Shenyang
    - New World Dept. Store
    - Charter Times Square
    - Seibu
28. Shenzhen
    - Mix City
    - Seibu Dept. Store
    - Yitian Holiday Plaza
29. Shijiazhuang
    - Fortune Mall
30. Suzhou
    - Matro Fashion Town

31. Taiyuan
    - Tian Mei
32. Taizhou
    - Zhong Sheng
      Dept. Store
33. Tianjin
    - Hisense
    - Friendship Store
34. Urumqi
    - Dan Lu Dept. Store
    - Ginwa Dept. Store
35. Wenzhou
    - Wenzhou Intime
    - Wenzhou Times Square
36. Wuhan
    - New World Dept. Store
    - Wuchang New World
      Dept. Store
37. Wuxi
    - New World
      Dept. Store
38. Xiamen
    - Xindeco Market
39. Xi'an
    - Ginwa Department Store
    - Chang On Ctr.
40. Xuzhou
    - Golden Eagle
41. Yantai
    - Baihong
42. Zhengzhou
    - Holiday Inn
    - Zheng Hong Dept. Store
    - Zhenzhou Xinmate

FIGURE 1: *Dunhill outlets in China, 2009*

Recognizing the difference in China's consumption patterns, dunhill's mainland offerings included a wide range of more casual wear: belts, polos, shirts, trousers and overcoats, in addition to formal tailoring.

In 2006, dunhill announced the company's next step for development in China, acquiring its business from China Resources (Holdings) Co. Ltd., its largest franchisee (managing, at the time, 25 dunhill stores including those in Beijing, Shanghai, Guangzhou, Shenzhen, Nanjing, Shenyang, Dalian, Changchun, and Harbin). Other (second and third tier) cities with dunhill sales points have kept business as usual with original franchisees on a case-by-case basis. An article published in the *China Daily* in 2006 cites China as dunhill's second-largest market, behind Japan and ahead of the United Kingdom. According to Alfred Dunhill China's managing Director, Jonathan Seliger, dunhill takes a "two-pronged approach to building distribution in China. While we continue to internalize strategic cites from legacy franchisees, we also promote our local partners to explore opportunities in fast-developing second and third tier cites that are now ready for luxury brands. At the same time, our retail business continues to expand in large first and second tier cities, opening larger flagship stores in key shopping malls, for example our Brand Home in Shanghai."

Richemont

In September 2008, Richemont reported that sales for dunhill's Leather & Accessories department were up 2%, with high single-digit sales in Asia-Pacific partly offsetting lower sales in Japan. Menswear was up 7% following the appointment of Kim Jones as Creative Director, and the opening of Alfred Dunhill homes in Shanghai, Tokyo, and London. In comparison to Richemont's other businesses, dunhill's performance in the Asian market was remarkable.

In its 2008 Annual Report, the Richemont group recorded mainland China sales totaling US$320 million—5% of its worldwide sales—with profitability in line with the group average. With offices in Beijing and Shanghai, it had 530 staff across its 14 *maisons* (fully-owned customer-service centers), 166 boutiques and 340 points of sale for watches in 60 mainland cities.

Worldwide, dunhill saw losses amounting to US$12 million in the first half of 2007/08. Despite low sales, the Asia-Pacific region was cited as contributing 60% of all dunhill sales, which we estimate at around US$400 million (an increase at a constant rate of 9%). Despite the effects of a sharp decline in the Shanghai Stock Exchange in 2008, dunhill's operations in China grew by 8% and in so doing contributed 24% of the company's worldwide sales.

Dunhill currently employs more than 1,000 people worldwide across 180 stores and 3,500 wholesale and retail sales points in five main regions: Europe, Asia Pacific, China, Japan, and the United States. The vast majority of store openings and renovations in recent times have been in Asia.

Business model

Having investments that create long-term value and cash flow generation remain priorities for the Richemont group. Its primary business model is to have long-term value creation with priority given to organic growth, and a coherent and promising portfolio of all *maisons*, or houses. Its main priorities for 2009 are to maintain its product and distribution channel mix in Asia-Pacific and emerging markets, and to focus on generating cash flow.

In addition, a focus on ready-to-wear has become key, given that sales for menswear are heavily dependent on sales of leather goods. Apparel sales has also been incredibly strong in Asia-Pacific markets such as Korea. An advertising campaign aimed exclusively at the

Asian market (including China, Hong Kong and Taiwan) features the Oscar-nominated actor Jude Law.

Main competitors

The company's main international competitors include other British menswear brands such as Burberry, Paul Smith, Savile Row tailors Gieves & Hawkes, or Thomas Pink. Italian houses Ermenegildo Zegna and Giorgio Armani—both famous for their business suits and casual attire—are likely to pose greater threats. In the Chinese market, all of the aforementioned have a strong presence, and are further matched by domestic brands such as Ports 1961's menswear line (only available in China), Hugo Boss, local tailors with long histories such as those found on Maoming Road in Shanghai, and even Richemont's own Shanghai Tang, which boasts its own service for custom-tailored menswear and is home to an invitation-only Mandarin Collar Society for men.

Collaboration and events

Alfred Dunhill began to sponsor events most actively in the 1980s. Perhaps its most famous annual event is the Alfred Dunhill Links Championship (which began life as the Alfred Dunhill Cup in 1985), a part of the European PGA Tour, an international team golf competition played on the famous old Scottish links courses at St. Andrews, Carnoustie and Kingsbarns. Each year, the event attracts a host of celebrities from the worlds of sport, show-business and entertainment. However, not all dunhill events occur on such a grand scale. One notable boutique event included the "Alfred Dunhill Debate" which took place during the opening of the New York flagship store. Highlighting the contentious issue of the "United States versus the United Kingdom," it pitted pro-American Donny Deutsch—of CNBC's show *The Big Idea*—against pro-Britain Piers Morgan. The evening was attended by more than a hundred high-profile Americans and British expats.

As a producer of luxury leather goods, dunhill has also collaborated with luxury car manufacturer Bentley to create exclusive leather luggage. The partnership also allowed for the exclusive use of Bentley cars at the dunhill Homes in London, and Shanghai for VIP customers. A chauffeur service is also found at each home, complete with Bentley Continental Flying Spurs. In 2006, dunhill joined with the Forpeople design group to launch a series of premium products and accessories such as the *Revolette* pen, an anniversary edition of the Rollagas lighter, and PlayStation PSP pouches.

Summary

Dunhill's history in producing luxury goods and garments for men, and the brand's current visibility and accessibility in the industry have come together to legitimize the brand for Chinese consumers, with new designs, products, and markets. With Kim Jones (voted Menswear Designer of the Year by the British Fashion Council in 2006) on board, dunhill is beginning to break its traditional mold, as evidenced by the British Luxury Overseas Award for Excellence it received at the 2008 Walpole Awards, beating out competitors such as Thomas Pink and other luxury brands such as Vertu and Bentley.

The *New York Times* recently pointed out how mid-level clothing lines have become all the rage—"recession destinations"—during the current financially tough times, when the majority of people tend not make a purchase unless it is an absolute necessity. The world economic crisis and its subsequent push for consumers to become increasingly frugal poses a definite threat to dunhill and the rest of the luxury industry. The biggest obstacle dunhill has to face is to convince consumers that money is worth spending and that its products—above all else—possess a high value for Chinese consumers.

Major issues

Alfred Dunhill suffers from the strong presence and performance of its tobacco license business worldwide. This business is run by the British American Tobacco Company and exported throughout Europe, the Middle East, South Asia, South Africa, New Zealand and Australia. Its products are also found on the Internet and in tobacconists throughout North America and Malaysia. This creates confusion among consumers about the brand image and positioning. Alfred Dunhill is a man's brand; it retains a strong association with older generations of smokers. How the company resolves the problem will be a key issue, although it does actively distance the luxury business from any association with cigarettes.

For many years, Alfred Dunhill has had the problem of brand aging in the mainland China market. Like Mercedes-Benz, Rolex and the 555 cigarette brand, it has a huge reputation in China because of its presence in the early stages of China's opening policy. And at that time there were very few international brands in China. Imported luxury goods could be afforded only by the very rich and the very powerful and thus created a tremendous reputation in the minds of Chinese consumers. But times have changed and the older generation of wealthy people has gradually been replaced by newer wealth from the internet boom and a globalized environment.

Yet the image of Alfred Dunhill hasn't changed much for more than 15 years and retains its strong association with tobacco products. How to attract younger wealthy Chinese consumers is a crucial issue for dunhill in China.

Facing strong competition from Ermenegildo Zegna and Armani in menswear and surrounded by a proliferation of media messages, dunhill has to find its specific positioning in the Chinese luxury market. To do this, it has to revitalize the brand and refresh its identity to attract the younger consumers and today's rising stars. This would be in line with the way people value success in China and the way they judge people and brands. The marketing emphasis should be on communication and marketing activities that target the elite consumer with the message that dunhill is made for rising stars.

To maintain its historical high-end positioning, the company should maximize the usage of the Dunhill Homes to develop private clubs for the elite consumer, promoting the Homes of dunhill as the perfect place for them to share great moments with friends and business partners.

It should continue to improve the landmark location of its retailing network along the lines of its flagship stores in Shanghai and Beijing's luxury landmarks, and combine its branding activities to create a unique service and brand experience.

ENDNOTE

1　This case study was compiled from public and online sources by Elizabeth Peng, U.S. Fulbright Scholar to China, under the direction of Professor Pierre Xiao Lu. It is intended for educational use and as a basis for discussion, and does not represent a model for handling any managerial situation.

CHAPTER 2

The Chinese Luxury Client

W HO BUYS luxury products in China? In a developing country of more than 1.3 billion inhabitants and with many individuals living below the subsistence level, the question is certainly necessary. It is true that China is changing, but not always as fast as people think and the changes are not necessarily applicable to a country where per-capita GNP was still as low as US$865 in 2007, ranking 108th in the world.

Who are the Chinese luxury clients?

The very rich

In their annual World Wealth Report for 2008, Cap Gemini and Merrill Lynch define the category of high-net-worth individuals as those who have at least US$1 million in financial assets, and reports that China had 415,000 such individuals (out of a total of 2.8 million in Asia), up from 345,000 the previous year, or an increase of 20%. This new wealth is also reflected in the fact that by the end of 2007, the Shanghai stock market had the sixth-largest total market capitalization in the world.

What is interesting about these high-net-worth individuals is the way they consider spending their money, as outlined in Table 2.1.

TABLE 2.1: *Spending patterns of high-net-worth individuals*

	Europeans	North Americans	Asians
Luxury products[1]	33%	41%	47%
Luxury collectibles[2]	17%	17%	14%
Art collections	22%	11%	13%
"Wellness"[3]	9%	13%	15%
Others	19%	18%	11%
Total	100%	100%	100%

(1) Includes luxury consumables, luxury and experimental travel and jewelry, gems and watches.
(2) Includes automobiles, boats, jets, etc.
(3) Includes sports, saunas, clubs, travels, vacations, etc. Products such as cosmetics and make-up are
    included in the first group.
Source: Cap Gemini Merrill Lynch World Wealth Report, 2008

The affluent

But the very rich alone are not creating the growth of the Chinese luxury market to its present US$13 billion level. Probably a more important group is that of the affluent, defined in a joint study by Mastercard and HSBC[1] as those earning more than US$25,000 a year. In 2005, there were some 2.9 million individuals reported in this group, a figure expected to reach 8.5 million by 2015.

Table 2.2 shows a breakdown of the various income classes and the projections for their expected growth. Table 2.3 shows their principal locations.

It is important to note that a large part of middle-class income is used to purchase basic necessities. On the other hand, the discretionary spending of the affluent is quite large and growing very fast. It is forecast to move from US$17.7 billion in 2005 to US$117.4 billion in 2015.

Table 2.4 presents a profile of the affluent, who tend to be young (86% are below the age of 47), university graduates (in 83% of cases), almost half of whom have have considerable experience studying or working overseas, generally in the United States, the United Kingdom and Canada. Some 15% have had an overseas education and 17% travel abroad frequently, generally in Asia, but also in Europe (25% of last outbound travel) and in North America (13%).

TABLE 2.2: *China's middle class and the affluent, 2007*

	Population in 2005	Population in 2015	Discretionary spending as a percentage of total income
Middle class (income US$6,000 to US$25,000)	87 million	317 million	35%
Affluent (income over US$25,000)	2.9 million	8.5 million	75%

Note: The figures in this table should be used very carefully. At a first reading, they indicate that only 2.9 million Chinese citizens have an annual salary above US$25,000. In a country where people are now buying eight million cars every year (including many Mercedes, Audis and Porsche Cayenne) this seems difficult to believe. These are the "official" figures. In 2009, however, we assume that there are probably more than three million Chinese citizens with an income above US$130,000 a year. Only part of this comes from salaries; the rest comes in the form of gifts and from individual private activities. Nevertheless, the figures used in the table still have the advantage of structuring the different Chinese groups in a comprehensive manner.
Source: From Mastercard/HSBC point study on China Affluent, 2007

TABLE 2.3: *Location of the affluent, 2005 and 2015 (in 000s)*

	Location in 2005		Location in 2015		Growth
	total	%	total	%	%
Shanghai	607	20.9%	2,100	24.7%	245%
Beijing	279	9.6%	977	11.5%	250%
Guangzhou	240	8.3%	867	10.2%	260%
Others	1,774	61.2%	4,556	53.3%	156%
Total	2,900	100.0%	8,500	100.0%	193%

Source: From Mastercard/HSBC joint study on China Affluent, 2007

TABLE 2.4: *Profile of the affluent*

Age		Gender		Education		Overseas living and working experience	
Under 30	22%	Male	76%	No High School	1%	Yes	46%
31–46	64%	Female	24%	High School Graduate	5%	No	54%
Over 46	14%	Total	100%	College Graduate	11%	Total	100%
Total	100%			University Graduate	50%		
				Master's and above	33%		
				Total	100%		

Source: From Mastercard/HSBC joint study on China Affluent, 2007

In 40% of the cases, the affluent have overseas ties, with family members living abroad.

The affluent tend to work across a wide range of activities, with 10–15% each in manufacturing, finance, information technology and consulting. Of the total, 43% say they hold a senior position and all own real estate (with 65% owning two properties and 26% owning three properties).

As might be expected, the attitude of the affluent towards luxury products is quite positive. Table 2.5 summarizes their feelings, and it is interesting to note that 48% of them give the quality of goods as their primary motivation for buying a luxury product.

Of course, the mention of quality is an easy disguise for perhaps other, more personal, motivations. But as this affluent group expands to the projected 8.5 million individuals over the next few years, it holds out interesting possibilities for the future of the luxury business.

The middle class

A separate—more detailed—study, undertaken by the Chinese Academy of Social Sciences,[2] set the financial qualification for a middle-class household at RMB75,000 (equivalent to US$6,000; that is, at the lower end of the scale used in the first study). By this

TABLE 2.5: *Motivation for purchasing luxury goods*

Good quality	48%
Pampering self	16%
Status symbol	14%
Trendy	14%
Investment	2%
Recommended	2%
As a means to acquire a foreign culture	1%
No answer; don't know	3%
	100%

Source: HSBC China affluent study, 2007

measure, in 2005 some 105 million individuals—19% of the urban population—came into this category. What makes this impressive is not so much the figures themselves as the fact that in 2001 this category represented only 1% of the urban population. If the present growth (an additional 20–25 million individuals a year) continues, this category will have expanded to 200 million in 2009.

This group represents a total income of approximately US$1,000 billion, making it equivalent in size to the British or French markets. When the figures are adjusted to take account of purchasing price parity, this group has a total purchase potential three or four times larger in volume than the markets of Britain, Germany, France and Italy combined.

In their use of household equipment, this group could be compared to European households in the 1990s. They all have fixed and portable telephones, a washing machine, a refrigerator, a color television and air-conditioning systems—and often more than one of each. While for the vast majority the main mode of personal transport is the bicycle, 27% of them own a motorcycle and 11% own a car.

It is in this group that we might expect a gradual increase in purchases of perfumes, wines and spirits, and, occasionally, luxury watches and handbags.

A research project conducted by CLSA China Reality Research in 2007 looked at a population of 59 million middle-class Chinese consumers. Their saving and spending patterns are set out in Table 2.6.

TABLE 2.6: *Saving and spending among China's middle class*

Breakdown of income		Breakdown of spending	
Saving	20%	Groceries	23%
Spending	80%	Children's education	15%
		Housing	10%
		Clothing	8%
Total:	100%	Transport	6%
		Healthcare	5%
		Others	13%
		Total:	100%

Source: CLSA China Reality Research, summer 2007

The first striking finding is, of course, the large percentage of savings among the Chinese middle class: this is because the social security systems and retirement plans are not very strong. People claim they save to buy their house (35%), for healthcare and retirement (33%) and for their children's education (24%).

The fact that housing represents only 10% of middle-class spending requires some explanation. In fact, 60% of them own their home (compared, for example, to 40% in Germany). But of the total middle-class population, 26% live in a parent's home, and 31% own a house that they either paid for in cash or have paid off entirely. Thus, 57% either live in the family home or in a fully paid home of their own, which gives these people additional spending power.

Differences in the luxury consumer profile

As mentioned earlier, times are changing in China and with them the purchasing patterns of Chinese consumers. As Emmanuel Prat, president of LVMH Japan, observed in 2006: "men have been the traditional buyers and in 2001, three out of four consumers were men. Now, as more women are becoming economically independent, they account for a larger share of the luxury market and there is a big potential."[3] However, while the balance is undoubtedly shifting, men are likely to continue to exercise the dominant influence in this sphere for some time to come. The reason for this is twofold: men manage the household budget; and it is estimated that half of luxury purchasing in China takes the form of "business gifts"—for employees on a special occasion or for outstanding performance; for customers or for business associates.

The findings were confirmed by another study, conducted by KPMG consultants, Australia's Monash University and the TNS market research firm, which found that: "Until recently, 90% of all luxury spending in China was dictated by men." However, it also observed that "young Chinese women are beginning to supplant business men aged over 35 as the main buyers of luxury goods. . . .

[T]he modern female luxury shopper includes the business woman, the celebrity and the newly independent rich wife."[4]

Obviously, women—particularly younger women—will one day become the major clients of luxury goods in China. The younger generation is undoubtedly emerging as the buying power for super brands, as John Chaltok from KPMG Shanghai has pointed out: "In urban China, studies estimated that more than 50% of the one-child family's disposable income is spent on or by its youngest member, who knows what he wants, expects the best and is not shy about asking for it."[5] Though the movement towards younger and more feminine customers is undoubtedly under way, it remains to be seen how long this process will take to complete.

It is clear, then, that it is still a comparatively small group of the very rich, the affluent and occasional middle-class "excursionists" who continue to make up the bulk of luxury purchasing. On the basis of Table 2.3, the best market target would appear to be Shanghai but it should not be forgotten that Beijing is home to many very powerful corporations (For a more detailed analysis of these two cities, see Appendix B.)

Chinese attitudes towards luxury goods

The following section is based on a 2007 study of affluent consumers,[6] who were defined in two categories: the **mass affluent**, with an annual household income of between US$16,000 and US$50,000; and the **rich**, with an annual household income above US$50,000. Here, we will concentrate on the findings relating to their travel patterns and their social and family values.

Travel patterns of the affluent

The study showed that 48% of the affluent travel abroad every year and 30% travel more than three times per year. Their destinations vary according to whether they live in Beijing, Shanghai or Guangzhou, as Table 2.7 shows.

TABLE 2.7: *Most frequent destinations of affluent Chinese*

Beijing		Shanghai		Guangzhou	
Hong Kong	79%	Hong Kong	75%	Hong Kong	90%
America	34%	Singapore	31%	Macau	49%
Singapore	15%	Japan	25%	Thailand	13%
Thailand	10%	Macau	14%	Singapore	11%
Japan	10%	America	13%	Japan	11%
Macau	7%	Thailand	11%	America	9%

Source: China Economic Monitoring and Analysis Center: "Lifestyle Report for Chinese Affluent Households," June 2007

Hong Kong is the most frequent destination for all, with Macau, the United States and Singapore also featuring strongly. The net profile is that more than 50% of the affluent travel regularly to Hong Kong and Macau, over 30% visit Thailand and Singapore, and between 12% and 20% visit Japan, Malaysia and South Korea. Whatever their city of residence, 10.5% visit Australia, 9.4% France, 8.4% Germany and 5.8% Italy in a given year.

Their domestic travel includes both business and leisure purposes. For the latter, the focus is mainly in natural landscapes (46%), cultural and historical sites (23%) and beach resorts (14%).

Family values of the affluent

Table 2.8 summarizes the attitudes held by the affluent towards family and work activities.

TABLE 2.8: *Family values of the affluent*

0: I strongly disagree—5: I strongly agree	
A happy family life is the most important for me	4.46
I attend entertainment activities together with my family as often as possible	4.19
I choose to give up my leisure time to promote my work performance	3.06
I choose to reduce or give up my leisure time to earn more money	2.61

Source: China Economic Monitoring and Analysis Center: "Lifestyle report for China's affluent households," June 2007.

What is striking here is that affluent respondents answer in about the same way as an American or European would have done, maybe with a stronger emphasis here on the improvement of work performance.

Attitudes towards luxury products

This section draws on a report published by KPMG–TNS in 2008[7] and is based on a survey of 902 middle-class respondents from 15 different cities. Respondents had an annual income above US$3,250 in the smaller cities and US$4,500 in Beijing, Shanghai, Guangzhou and Shenzhen. While this study's income benchmarks were considerably lower than in the other studies, it is probably the most interesting because it speaks of "individuals" rather than "households" and also interviewed people from the western part of the country. It is also very important as it mainly deals with attitudes rather than behavior, and enables us to understand how Chinese customers react to luxury products.

Table 2.9 indicates the levels of brand recognition and compares results from a study of 2006.

TABLE 2.9: *Brand recognition level for middle-class Chinese (aided recall)*

	Clothes	Bags & Shoes	Watches	Jewelry	Imported cars	Others	TOTAL
Number of brands in list (2006)	36	15	25	9	17	67	169
Average number recognized in 2006	9.3	4.7	7.6	2.5	10.1	17.5	51.7
Number of brands in list (2008)	37	33	24	11	17	75	197
Average number recognized in 2008	10.5	12.4	8.2	3.5	11.1	18.2	63.9

Source: KPMG–TNS

From this, it is fairly clear that more than 30% of the brands mentioned by the interviewers were known to the Chinese middle class, with similar results for 2006 and 2008. Cars, with 65%, commanded the highest degree of recognition (at least in percentage terms); bags and shoes had 37% recognition and watches had 34%. These figures are probably on a par with Japan and certainly much higher than in, say, Germany.

It is also interesting to note that brand awareness (in average-number terms) for bags and shoes developed very rapidly from 2006 to 2008, while there was very little difference in, say, watches over that same period.

It is interesting, too, to consider the kinds of goods that interested the respondents and their reasons for buying them, as summarized in the following four tables:

TABLE 2.10: *"I am willing to pay a premium for luxury goods with a long heritage"*

Annual income (RMB)	Very willing	Willing	TOTAL
Over 96,000 (US$7,500)	33%	45%	78%
72,000–96,000 (US$5,500–7,500)	37%	39%	76%
Under 72,000 (US$5,500)	27%	40%	67%

Source: KPMG–TNS

TABLE 2.11: *"I am willing to pay a premium for a positive retail experience"*

Gender	Very willing	Willing	TOTAL
Female	27%	40%	67%
Male	20%	40%	60%

Source: KPMG–TNS

TABLE 2.12: *"I am willing to pay a premium for goods that are fashionable"*

Age	Very willing	Willing	TOTAL
35–44	24%	39%	63%
30–34	13%	36%	49%
25–29	14%	32%	46%
20–24	13%	50%	63%

Source: KPMG–TNS

TABLE 2.13: *"I am willing to pay a premium for goods of European or North American origin"*

	Very willing	Willing	TOTAL
Goods of North American origin	3%	15%	18%
Goods of European origin	8%	25%	33%

Source: KPMG–TNS

These responses indicate that Chinese consumers, like their Japanese counterparts, are interested in a brand's heritage, are attracted by fashionable items and are looking for a special retail experience.

The fact that these brands come from Europe or North America plays a small part in the overall appreciation of the brands. It may be part of the long heritage and history of a given brand but, in itself, this is not enough to justify paying a premium price.

But why would middle-class Chinese buy or consider buying luxury products? Part of the answer is given in Table 2.14, which describes their different motivations.

TABLE 2.14: *Motivation for buying luxury goods*

To reflect my personality	Beijing	49%
	Shanghai	50%
To reflect taste and discernment	Beijing	50%
	Shanghai	47%
To pamper myself	Beijing	47%
	Shanghai	52%
To stand out from the masses	Beijing	24%
	Shanghai	41%
Because I am a "connoisseur"	Beijing	18%
	Shanghai	16%

Source: KPMG–TNS

Putting all of this information together presents a clearer picture of Chinese middle-class consumers: they look for brand heritage and fashion content and purchases that will help reflect their personality, taste and discernment. But what is the general view regarding those who buy or own luxury products? Respondents in the research survey generally had a favorable view of such people, the vast majority seeing them as successful and having good taste. Only a small minority viewed them as being "flashy" or wasteful. The results are recorded in Table 2.15.

TABLE 2.15: *Attitudes towards people who own luxury brands*

They are successful	64%
They have good taste	53%
They are fashionable	28%
They are show-offs flashy	18%
They are "nouveau riche"	14%
They are wasting money	14%
They are superficial	3%

Source: Chinese Luxury Consumers, 2008

Chinese shopping patterns

Shopping in China

The Chinese shopper is quite different from other shoppers. In a 2007 ACNielsen study, one-third of mainland respondents said clothes shopping was their favorite thing to do. This is the highest percentage in the world, and 20% higher than the world average. In the same study, 34% of respondents said they would go shopping just for entertainment once a week. In the specific case of Hong Kong, the study found that 93% said they would go shopping even if they did not plan to buy anything.

THE CHINESE LUXURY CLIENT 41

It might also be interesting to know how middle-class Chinese consumers get around. Table 2.16 gives some indication of the modes of transport they use.

TABLE 2.16: *Main forms of transport of the Chinese middle class*

Bus or subway	59%
By foot	23%
Electric bicycle	23%
Taxi	19%
Regular bicycle	17%
Motorcycle	14%
Private car	8%
Company bus	6%
Company car	2%

Source: CLSA China Reality Research, summer 2007

Of those who own a private car, 59% paid in cash and only 41% bought on credit.

As most people travel by bus, subway or taxi, shopping is done in the center of the cities.

Another survey has shown that the Chinese spend more time shopping than anybody else (see Tables 2.17 and 2.18).

TABLE 2.17: *Hours per week spent on shopping*

China	9.3
United States	3.6
France	3.0

TABLE 2.18: *Shops visited per week*

China	4.6
United States	3.1
France	2.5

Source: "How half the world shops in 2006," Shanghai Daily, August 2, 2007

One could, of course, explain the number of shops visited by the fact that in China there are still a large number of individual stores and shopping is rarely done in a single supermarket or department. But the number of hours spent is almost three times more than in the United States or in France. Obviously, Chinese people like shopping and this is probably another reason why they are so interested in luxury brands. They are actively looking for information about different brands. Affluent Chinese, for example, use the different sources of information indicated in Table 2.19.

While retail stores are the major source of information, fashion magazines, word of mouth and the internet are other important sources and this points up the need for, and the potential of, greater PR activity.

TABLE 2.19: *Information sources used by affluent Chinese*

Fashion magazines	63%
Business magazines	46%
Retail stores	42%
Word of mouth	32%
Television	26%
Newspapers	13%
Company/Brand webpage	12%
POS introduction	9%
Third-party webpage	6%
Billboard advertising	6%

Source: Master Card/HSBC Joint study on the Chinese affluent, 2007

Shopping abroad

Like any other luxury customers in the world, Chinese consumers take advantage of their trips abroad to buy luxury products, particularly in duty-free areas. In their study of the affluent, KPMG–TNS addressed this point and Table 2.20 shows the split between luxury goods purchased in China and those purchased overseas.

TABLE 2.20: *Luxury goods purchased by the affluent, domestically and overseas*

Purchase location	Total	More than once a year	Once a year	Once every two years	Less than once every two years
Mainland China only	57%	14%	36%	61%	64%
Overseas only	7%	7%	5%	6%	10%
Mainland China and overseas	36%	79%	59%	33%	26%
	100%	100%	100%	100%	100%

Source: Adapted from KPMG–TNS, 2008

People who seldom buy luxury goods (less than once every two years) make most of their purchases (64%) in China and seldom overseas (26+10 = 36). On the other hand, frequent purchasers (more than once a year) only rarely make their purchases domestically (14%).

The potential of the affluent Chinese who travel is enormous. The majority (59%) of those who travel abroad take advantage of their trips to buy luxury goods for their friends. But the numbers are staggering. As Antoine Colonna, from Merrill Lynch Paris pointed out in 2004, "There are 25 million Chinese traveling now and there will be 100 million in 2020, with each spending an average of US$1,000 per trip."[8] Elisabeth Ponsolle Des Portes, CEO of the Paris Comité Colbert, had a similar message in 2008, when the Paris department store Galeries Lafayette reported that for some luxury brands 30% of their sales came from Chinese tourists.[9]

Conclusion

The Chinese luxury market today is still male-dominated, with business gifts continuing to make a substantial contribution. The current balance is very likely to change in the near future because the general population has a very positive attitude toward luxury brands, a strong interest in fashion and what seems to be a compulsive need to go shopping.

ENDNOTES

1   Mastercard/HSBC joint study on China's Affluent, 2007.
2   Quoted in UBIFRANCE, "le modèle de consommation Chinois," May 18, 2007.
3   Quoted in *Shanghai Daily*, November 3, 2006.
4   Ibid.
5   "Young drive spending on luxuries," Zhang Fengming, *Shanghai Daily*, November 30, 2006.
6   China Economic Monitoring and Analysis Center, "Lifestyle report for Chinese affluent households," June 2007.
7   KPMG–TNS, "China's Luxury Consumers, moving up the curve," Nick Debman, KPMG China and George Svinos, KPMG Australia, 2008.
8   In Thomas 2007: 306.
9   Jacoberger-Lavoué 2008.

Shanghai Tang[1]

David Tang first opened the Hong Kong-based Shanghai Tang in 1994. He began the brand as a custom-tailoring fashion house that preserved the artistic talents of Shanghainese tailors who had fled Communist China. The Hong Kong boutique attracted over a million visitors within its first year. In 1996, Tang expanded the brand into the ready-to-wear field before selling a majority share to Swiss luxury group Richemont the following year.

In 1997, David Tang had attempted what turned out to be a short-lived venture on Madison Avenue, with an ostentatious opening event complete with celebrity sightings and performances. The concept of the store itself was to have been a "tongue-in-cheek, postmodern take on the styles and artifacts of China's recent past—with Madison Avenue prices and decidedly untraditional colors like hot pink and neon green."[2] After 19 months, and despite sales rumored to be in the region of US$18 million, the flagship closed. The company subsequently relocated its New York branch to more modest surroundings.

The product

In 2001, the company's new executive chairman, Raphael le Masne de Chermont, brought in Joanne Ooi as Creative Director and together they set about revamping the brand's image and design, working to develop the brand's image while maintaining its philosophy. They began focusing on women's ready-to-wear and, after much experimentation, decided that each collection should reflect a China-related theme, beginning with the Spring/Summer 2008 collection, which had the Silk Road as its theme.

Indeed, all the company's product offerings—from clothing for men, women and children, home furnishings, accessories, gifts and so on—were to reflect its Chinese cultural roots. While many of these items are also sold through its online shop, the luxury items are sold only in stores. Its made-to-measure Imperial Tailoring Service—conducted in a traditional salon setting reminiscent of Shanghai in the 1930s and reflecting the motto "the apogee of the Chinese Art of Living and Chinese Creativity"—carries the time-honored traditions of Shanghainese tailoring into the 21st century, with all embroidery, beading, sequins, and signature Chinese fastenings being hand-stitched. It also hosts trunk shows for bridal, formal, outwear, and men's suits twice a year in Shanghai Tang flagship stores in London, New York, and Singapore.

In 2007, the company introduced what it calls "The Mandarin Collar Society," with the stated aim being to "liberate men from the necktie." The Society revolves around a limited number of carefully chosen "MCS Ambassadors," hand-picked for their pre-eminence in their respective fields. These include British sprint champion Linford Christie, Michelin star chef Pierre Gagnaire, and internationally acclaimed pianist Lang Lang. Abiding by the "Mandarin Collar Society Manifesto," the founding members have exclusive access to made-to-measure products, impeccable service counters for MCS at the company's flagship stores in Hong Kong, New York, London, and Singapore.

Shanghai Tang has a boutique at Caesar's Palace in Las Vegas and, in December 2008, opened its first Spanish boutique in Madrid. Its vision is to have 50 sales points around the world by 2010.

Development in China

Though undoubtedly successful with tourists, Shanghai Tang's flagship in Hong Kong suffers from the perception among the Chinese that the store is predominantly geared towards foreigners. Another problem for Shanghai Tang has been to sell the "made-in-China" tag to its very own Chinese consumers, who tend to prefer Western luxury houses such as Hugo Boss, Armani, or dunhill. It attempts to differentiate itself from other luxury houses by not limiting itself to the term "luxury brand" but, rather, presents itself as a premium brand with luxury principles.

The team at Shanghai Tang has also made sure that its new boutiques have steered clear of trying to recreate the deliberately nostalgic ambience and period furniture of the Hong Kong flagship store.

The company has recognized that there is no need to tweak the brand to suit the mainland Chinese, who still prefer Western-style fashion and trends. The Mandarin Collar Society, which promotes Chinese-style fashions, is an attempt to reach out to Chinese consumers, ensuring the future success of Shanghai Tang. However, its products are 25% more expensive in China than in Hong Kong. With such pricing, these products are, in the eyes of Chinese mainlanders, more geared towards foreign tourists than to local Chinese. This view tends to be reinforced by the fact that all Shanghai Tang's stores are located in five-star hotels, in tourist districts, and in airport duty-free stores.

However, Shanghai Tang does appeal to mainland Chinese who have international exposure and to the overseas Chinese themselves, who wish to convey their roots, identity and values through fashions that combine a mix of Western and Eastern cultures.

Shanghai Tang's success is due in part to the strength of the Asian market, which is responsible for 80 percent of the brand's sales. Its standing and prospects in China received a considerable boost in 2004 when it became the first company from outside the mainland to be admitted to the China Trademark Association, China's most exclusive business club, which represents the nation's leading 300 brands.

Shanghai Tang currently has 12 stores in China (see Table 1), and is looking to launch a chain of cafés.

TABLE 1: *Shanghai Tang stores in mainland China*

Beijing	Beijing Capital International Airport, Intl. Departure Lounge, Gate No. 12 Beijing Capital International Airport, Intl. Departure Lounge, Terminal 3 Beijing Grand Hyatt Hotel Shop, 1 East Chang An Avenue Beijing Ritz Carlton Hotel China Central Place, 83A Jian Guo Road Beijing Yintai Centre Shop, 2 Jianguomenwai Street
Guangzhou	Guangzhou New Baiyun International Airport, International Terminal
Hangzhou	Hyatt Regency Hangzhou, 28 Hu Bin Road
Macau	Taipa Island, The Shoppes at Four Seasons Estrada da Baia de N. Senhora da Esperanca, Cotai Strip
Shanghai	Jin Jiang Hotel, 59 Mao Ming Nan Road Xintiandi Plaza, 15 Xintiandi North Block, Lane 181 Tai Cang Rd. Shangri-La Hotel, 33 Fu Cheng Road, Pudong Shanghai Pudong International Airport, Terminal 2, B1 Area

Shanghai Tang's Hong Kong Store
Copyright: Pierre Xiao Lu

Collaboration and events

Shanghai Tang collaborates quite regularly with charities and organizations and has had the Hong Kong Cancer Fund as its primary charity partner since 2005. It also sponsors the not-for-profit "Save China's Tigers" to raise awareness for the protection and conservation of the South China tiger and other endangered cat species. The proceeds from its limited-edition polo shirts featuring the endangered tiger are donated to the organization. Shanghai Tang supports the sport of polo, and showcased its Fu Zhi collection as title sponsor of the Shanghai Tang International Women's Polo Tournament 2008 at Singapore's Polo Club for the third straight year. It has also been actively encouraging the sport throughout the whole of Asia, reviving it in Mongolia (where the sport is said to have originated).

Major issues

The first real issue for Shanghai Tang is to define what it is and what it should be. Starting life as a Shanghainese souvenir shop in Hong Kong, it is viewed as a "luxury Chinese" ready-to-wear opportunity for foreigners.

Although Raphaël de Masne has expressed concern that the brand is perceived as a "foreigners' brand" by Chinese customers, you have to wonder why in 2009 eight of its 34 free-standing stores are located in the duty-free section of international airport terminals, and why two of these (in Guangzhou and Taipei) are in places where the company has no stores at all in the domestic market.

The concept of "Imperial tailoring," which requires fittings and between seven to 10 days' lead time, does not seem to be targeted to tourists, who generally stay two to three days in a given city. Is the idea here to target expatriates who have a special taste for everything that looks Chinese, but which is slightly adapted to them? Or is it geared to wealthy Chinese consumers?

The idea of Shanghai Tang coffee shops is a very interesting one. But who are the target customers? Is the company still thinking about the tourist market or is it trying to develop a local population base?

In the Richemont group's 2008 annual report, Shanghai Tang is listed under the "other businesses" category, which makes it difficult to ascertain its precise individual profitability. However, it is fair to assume that with sales which we estimate to be in the region of US$55 million, it is at least breaking even. This then gives rise to the question of whether investing in a new chain of coffee shops is the best use of its resources or whether it might be better to develop existing activities with new products and new stores. In other words, should it concentrate on existing businesses or should it develop new ventures and new concepts?

Which of its various activities is essential for the future of the business and where should the financial efforts be concentrated?

Another issue relates to the company's geographical develop-ment. After early trials in the United States and in the United Kingdom, it seems that Shanghai Tang is now concentrating its activities in Asia and Dubai, where 25 of its 34 stores are currently located. Obviously, this seems to be the strongest part of the business. But what should it do outside of Asia? Should it consider the United States (where it currently has stores in Hawaii, Las Vegas and Miami, as well as New York) as a priority or should it focus on Europe and its current locations in London, Paris and Madrid? Should it do both?

In its initial development in the United States, Shanghai Tang had its own stores, as well as shop-in-shops in department stores. The advantage of department stores is that they provide faster growth because new locations require less upfront investment. Can the Shanghai Tang concept, despite its diversity and its strength, fit in a department store environment or should it be developed only in free-standing stores? Could there be another merchandising concept, more limited in scope, with more targeted products that could be sold in department stores?

This may be a way to develop the business at a faster pace. But obviously if the business has had a double-digit growth rate for the last five years, maybe the question is not really necessary.

In short, then, the main issues facing Shanghai Tang relate to what products it should sell, to whom, where and in what environment.

ENDNOTES

1   This case study was written by Elisabeth Peng, Fulbright Fellow from Rice University, under the direction of Professor Pierre Xiao Lu. It is intended to be used as the basis of discussion rather than as a model for handling a management situation. The case was compiled from published sources.

2   Hays, Constance. "A Fashion Mistake On Madison Avenue; Humbling End for Shanghai Tang and Its Gaudy Take on Chinese Style," *New York Times*, August 19, 1999.

CHAPTER 3

Chinese Consumer Attitudes Toward Luxury[1]

THIS CHAPTER focuses on Chinese consumers' attitudes and behaviors toward luxury products. The analysis, based on the elite class in economic hubs such as Beijing, Shanghai, Guangzhou and Chongqing, is intended to identify who buys luxury products and why they buy them, the characteristics of their luxury consumption, and the implications of all this for luxury firms and marketers.

Conspicuous consumption and the Chinese elite

Conspicuous consumption

In China, the desire for high-quality, fine-design products is nothing new, having existed for many hundreds of years in the imperial court. The exchange of gifts between royal courts was common practice in Asia and Europe, where the owners and consumers of luxury goods had a similar profile. However, the discovery of a new continent and new trade routes, colonization, industrialization, two world wars, political evolutions and economic competition transformed relations between Asia and the West. In China, the traditional luxury industry and the famous artisans' ateliers were not able to survive and compete with their European counterparts. This is one of the reasons why there are very few traditional Asian luxury brands today, especially in China. But the interest in luxury products, and the conspicuousness which is associated with it, still remains.

In Western countries, conspicuousness is one of the important functions of luxury products and brands for the leisure class. As the effects of the Industrial Revolution in the late eighteenth and early nineteenth centuries spread from Great Britain to Europe, North America and the rest of the world, a new social class—the leisure class—emerged and introduced a bourgeois lifestyle. The hallmark of the ensuing social and economic transformation was the conspicuous behavior of the "nouveau riche" in displaying its wealth and status as a means of acquiring social respect.[2]

"Learning from Westerners" became common for Asian countries, with their contact with Western ideas and institutions. The first mover in this respect was Japan, which launched its Meiji Modernization at the end of the nineteenth century. After the Second World War, industrialization also boosted economic development in South Korea, Singapore, Taiwan and Hong Kong. People became wealthy, enjoying the modernization brought by Westerners. Western lifestyles became trendy and "*à la mode*" for the elite and young people. Western luxury products became symbols of success and social standing.

In Chinese-dominated societies such as Hong Kong, Taiwan and Singapore, the majority of today's citizens are descendants of war refugees, poor farmers and fishermen who fled poverty and deprivation in their native land to earn a living elsewhere. Once established, they began to buy luxury products to reflect their success and to gain social recognition and respect—much as their nineteenth-century European and American counterparts had done. In mainland China today, after decades of an opening and flexible economic policy, the country has entered into a period of transition (see Schütte and Ciarlante 1998) and a "new rich" class has emerged, bringing with it conspicuous consumption and many millions of luxury-product consumers.

The Chinese elite

Who belongs to the Chinese elite, the main target customer for luxury products? The economic reforms instigated by Deng Xiao Ping

TABLE 3.1: *Demographic and socioeconomic criteria to define elite*

Demographic criteria	Chinese Elite
Age	25–50 years old
Gender	Male and female
Region/Cities	Beijing, Tianjin, Shanghai, Guangzhou, Shenzhen . . . (mainland economic hubs)
Socioeconomic criteria	
Income	Average monthly personal income:[3] at least 10 times the national average income[4]
Occupational Status	Entrepreneurs, senior managers and successful professionals etc.
Education	Bachelor's degree is a minimum; most have a Master's degree

in 1979 have brought about the emergence of a new social class in economically developed urban areas—Beijing, Shanghai, Guangzhou, Shenzhen, Chengdu, Chongqing and so on. The evolving distribution of the social classes is not yet stabilized, which means that Chinese social classes are not yet as clearly differentiated as in American society, for example (see Schiffman and Kanuk 2001). Nevertheless, it is clear that something akin to Veblen's "leisure class" has emerged, along with an upper-middle class which could be named the "Chinese elite." Previous studies (Cui and Liu 2001; *Far Eastern Economic Review* 2002, for example), defined the Chinese elite by using criteria such as business profile (for example, CEO or senior manager), company operations (domestic or international), and personal profile (average age, university education or average monthly personal income). Based on these criteria, luxury consumers can be defined as shown in Table 3.1.

A new young elite is an obvious target for luxury goods, and this elite will be confronted with strong new ideology and Western values to be combined individually (or not) with traditional values. What are their attitudes and behavior with respect to luxury goods?

Luxury products: In-depth interviews and profiles

In-depth interviews with Chinese luxury consumers allowed us to pinpoint the main questions raised by the buying and consumption of luxury products. It is interesting to note that while all the consumers agreed that a luxury product should have very high brand awareness in addition to the usual characteristics of conspicuousness or excellent quality, they were not sensitive to the same aspects.

From the 22 in-depth interviews conducted, four types of consumers emerged: *luxury lovers, luxury followers, luxury intellectuals* and *luxury laggards*.

Luxury lovers know exactly what they want from luxury brands and products, and enjoy the conspicuousness of luxury. They are very oriented towards the conspicuous and are rational rather than impulsive in their purchasing.

Luxury followers are heavily influenced in their luxury choices by the trends created by the media, the brands and the public, rather than following their own feelings and understanding of luxury products and specific brands. They are clearly distinguished by three factors: they are collectivist, very conspicuous and very impulsive.

Luxury intellectuals have their own understanding of luxury and keep their distance from trends, preferring discreet and classical models of luxury brands. Their luxury consumption is very rational. They are individualistic and rational, and not very conspicuous in their consumption.

In general terms, *luxury laggards* don't care about luxury brands and products, although they can afford them. Their priority is functionality rather than the emotional side of a product. They are not influenced by advertising and are rational when it comes to pricing. However, they are impulsive, opportunistic buyers.

The lovers are the most sensitive to luxury innovations and *the laggards* are the least sensitive. Below, we give one example for each of these types, who display the contrasting characteristics of luxury consumers: conspicuousness versus functionality; collectivism versus individualism; price-impulsiveness versus analytical thinking.

The luxury lover

Wang Yan is a 29-year-old woman, recently married and without children. She graduated from People's University, majoring in media and communication studies. After four years' experience as a journalist and editor on a well-known newspaper, she enrolled in an MBA program at one of the most prestigious business schools in China. After graduating, she went into public relations and communication consultancy, working as a director in a U.S. consulting company in Beijing.

She is very energetic and open-minded, and very sensitive to luxury. She is a very successful business woman, with her own very clear understanding and vision of luxury. She always wears the most fashionable brands and likes to share her experiences with her friends, colleagues and business partners. All her clients are from the top 500 multinational companies, with very high levels of education and international experience. Her well-groomed appearance increases her credibility and raises her clients' trust in her business capabilities. Buying and owning luxury brands gives her the opportunity to share her insights on brands and luxury products with friends and peers. She reads high-end fashion magazines to keep up with the latest news about fashion and the luxury industry and to inform her purchasing decisions.

Her notions of luxury correspond with those a **luxury lover**. Her characteristics are **conspicuousness**, **analytical thinking** and **collectivism**.

> "I don't have a very strong attachment to a brand, but like new things which are very 'in' [luxury lover]. My order of priorities in luxury buying is cosmetics, clothes, bags, everything that can be seen. When a new luxury product is launched in China generally, I will try it . . . Once you have tried a better product, you will never move back to the old one. I choose a good product for myself . . . Now, I have four or five perfumes I like. These include 5th Avenue After 5 by Elizabeth Arden, J'adore by Christian Dior, and Envy by Gucci. Sometimes, I use Calvin Klein's neutral perfumes. And my favorite is a series of men's perfumes by Kenzo; it has a scent of bamboo leaves. It is a good product.

The bottle is like a lighter, the color is deep green. I use what I want; it depends on my mood. [Innovativeness].

My priority in luxury buying is everything that can be easily seen, such as bags, cars and watches. The brands should be recognized immediately. A luxury brand should have a long history, absolute quality guaranteed and a very high price. They should be aesthetic products accepted by lots of people. The brand's long history is a guarantee for consumers in terms of the quality and competence of the company. [Conspicuousness and collectivism]

Wearing luxury brands can give you confidence and convince others of your success in business; so the brand should be very famous and recognized by the people around you. [Collectivism]

I feel good with Lancôme. It is the most expensive among the brands in the same product category. So I feel that its products are better, and the logo is quite pretty too. I felt it was suitable for me, and so I used it.

My understanding of a brand is always from my own observation in magazines or on TV in my daily life. I never ask others to tell me what the brand is, except for digital products, where I need expert advice." [Analytical thinking]

The luxury follower

Zhang Yong is a 32-year-old married woman with a two-year-old son. She graduated from the Foreign Language Institute in Beijing, majoring in French literature, and received a Master's degree in management from UIBE. She is General Manager in a Sino-Belgian pharmaceutical joint-venture in Tianjin.

She is patient and kind, and gets along with all her friends and colleagues. She is a good listener and is easily influenced by others' ideas and perception. As the administrator of a company, she has lots of social activities, especially with government officials, business partners and clients. She pays attention to her appearance and follows fashion trends, wanting to be perceived as fashionable and successful.

Her luxury behavior corresponds with that of a **luxury follower**. She can be characterized as **collectivist, conspicuous, impulsive**.

> "I have a very strong follow-the-public mentality. My logic is: why is it so famous? It is because I can see it everywhere, the after-sales service is good, and the network of shops is everywhere, so it gives me a feeling of security that I can hold on to. Maybe you are a good brand, but if you have no after-sales services in Tianjin or Beijing, I don't dare buy it. [Follower, collectivism]

> For luxury products, the utility functions are far less important than the aesthetic functions. To possess the product is purely to be conspicuous and self-complacent. It can project to others a kind of visual happiness. I am a person who is easily influenced by advertisements. I will believe in the company or brand which can convince me. Of course, if it is a BMW, I will look at it more than others. For watches . . . I will always choose Longines. I think Longines' women watches are really very nice. For example, the model I have is super-thin, very popular. Of course Rolex women's watches are not very big either, but my colleagues all consider that Longines' super-thin model is the best." [Conspicuousness and collectivism]

For shoes, although they are much more expensive than in the domestic market, I prefer to buy them abroad, because obviously the style and quality are much better. For perfume, firstly, it is cheaper abroad; secondly, I like to buy it in the boutiques where there are test samples and the sales person can assist me in making a choice. If I like it, I will go for the brand. [Impulsive] In my bedroom I display different bottles of perfume, different brands, different bottle shapes, and different sizes. I like to use a different scent every day."

The luxury intellectual

Li Jing is a 31-year-old married woman with no children. She graduated as a dentist and, after five years' experience in a hospital, she and two partners started their own medical equipment company in Shanghai.

She is a very quiet and intellectual person who doesn't follow the trends and doesn't care about what other people think about her, relying instead on her own competencies and skills. She believes in facts and has built her reputation from the positive evaluation of her medical performance by her patients and peers.

Her thoughts on luxury correspond to those of a **luxury intellectual**, with **analytical, functional and individualist** characteristics.

"Buying a luxury product is to show social position and wealth; it stems from vanity for most people, for whom brand awareness is very important. But, for me, function and design are much more important. [Functional and individualist]

We just bought a car. It was a "new century elite" Santana from Volkswagen Shanghai. We needed it for going to the office and shopping, as it is economical and solid. Our house location was one element in deciding to buy a car. There is no public transport between my home and my office. But with a car, it takes only 15 minutes. I think this car corresponds well to our situation. But the most important point was it could improve our quality of life considerably. Personally, I like the Bluebird, but it costs much more in maintenance. This is a proven model and the customer-service network is very well managed. The decision process was quite long, because before we went to the dealer, we had already collected lots of information. We selected the model on the internet, so the final purchase was very fast. Because we already knew everything about the car, the final purchase was only a formality. When the sales person wanted to introduce another car model, I said we had already decided. [Analytical and functional]

I don't like bizarre styles and they must be relatively functional. I don't like bags which are too cheap or of poor quality either. [Functional]

I am not interested in cosmetics; I have no desire and demand for cosmetics. I don't care about how other people see me." [Individualist]

The luxury laggard

Liu Feng is a hard-working, 35-year-old married man. He holds a Bachelor's degree in engineering and an MBA. After working several years as IT director of an international company in Beijing, he started his own software company.

He has no sense of fashion and luxury, focusing instead on the technical side of a product. Because in his daily life he spends more time with computers than with people, he does not count on appearance to convince people and he has no opportunity for contact with fashion and luxury products and information. His success is built on his personal intelligence and hard work. He is an independent thinker and doesn't lay great store by the opinions of others. He is very sensitive to price, and brand name and luxury characteristics are a mere bonus.

His thoughts on luxury correspond to the characteristics of a **luxury laggard—functional, sensitive to price and promotion**.

"What is a luxury product? Having or not having the product in your life is not a big problem. It is not necessary for daily life. It is a symbol of social position.

I am very interested in digital products, where function is more important than price. [Functional] But as for my wife, she likes pretty things.

I bought a Pierre Cardin suit because a friend who works in the shop told me they had a sales promotion. So I went there and bought one at 50% discount. Without the discount, I would never have bought it. I don't care much about luxury things. [Individualist and sensitive to price]

I bought a Tissot watch, and a pair of Bally shoes during a discount period. I hadn't thought of buying the shoes but I saw the discount. My shoes were worn out and I needed a new pair, and these were OK for me because of the discount. So I bought them. [Impulsive and sensitive to price]

Price, quality, design, and brand are the priorities for me when choosing products. What I need is a functional product; the brand by itself is not important." [Functional]

From the interviews, it appears that three contrasting dimensions can be used to segment the market. These are:

- conspicuousness/functionality
- individualism/collectivism
- impulsiveness/analytical thinking

Dimensions to position luxury consumers

Conspicuousness/Functionality

Conspicuousness is related to values such as success and achievement, and to socially desirable goals such as wealth or social position. Achievement is strongly linked with conspicuous consumption (Belk 1985; Netemeyer, Burton and Lichtenstein 1995). In the Western context, the need for achievement is related to both the socially directed need for prestige and the personally directed need for self-actualization. People with a need for achievement tend to be more self-confident and enjoy taking calculated risks. They are very sensitive to new products or ventures, and are very interested in feedback. For Asian consumers, products and services that signify success are particularly appealing as they provide feedback about the realization of their goals and social recognition by others, which is even more important than for Westerners (Schütte and Ciarlante 1998). It is considered a glorious thing to be rich in modern Chinese society,[5] and this increases the Chinese desire to belong to a richer, higher class. Thus, social position is an important driver and motivation for luxury goods consumption.

But *economy, frugality, modesty and simplicity* are traditional Chinese virtues. In Chinese culture and history, a number of philosophers and scholars have expressed their opinions on such matters in articles long considered to be classical works. These include such sayings as: *"Frugality, the common point of virtue; luxury, the worst of sins"*[6] and *"Frugality and simplicity are beautiful."*[7] For many generations, aphorisms such as these were taught in schools and formed the basis of social ethics. Thus, from this "virtuous" viewpoint, the *functionality and simplicity* of a product are more highly valued than its conspicuousness.

Individualism/Collectivism

Individualism pertains to societies in which the ties between individuals are loose: everyone is expected to look after him/herself and their immediate family (Hofstede 1991). The Chinese elite generally live in large cities and have more opportunities for international exchange than the rest of the population. The influence of Western culture and international rules makes them rethink their behavior, and they have to adapt their thinking accordingly during such exchanges. The influence of individualism has become gradually more pervasive and affects their consumption behavior in ways that are at odds with the interdependence and collectivism of traditional Chinese society.

Interdependence/Collectivism has been defined as one of the main aspects of Chinese tradition that is possibly related to luxury consumption (see Wong and Ahuvia 1997). It is based on the fundamental connection of human beings to each other. Interdependence is a collectivist value. For the Chinese, class reflects not only the individual's achievement, but also the position of his family, relatives and kinship clan (Hsu 1981; Wong and Ahuvia 1997). The behavior of the individual should be guided by the expectations of the group. The chief moral system of China, Confucianism, was essentially an elaboration of the obligations between emperor and subject, parent and child, husband and wife, older brother and younger brother, and between friends. Such an emphasis on collective agency resulted in the Chinese valuing in-group harmony. Within the social group, any form of confrontation, such as debate, was discouraged. And a person could not contradict another without fear of making an enemy (Nisbett *et al.* 2001). This means that the collectivist consumer will be particularly sensitive to opinions expressed by other individuals and will tend to follow them.

Analytical/Impulsive Thinking (information-processing)

Personality influences attitudes towards consumption. Some individuals are impulsive and compulsive characters, easily influenced by advertising and the opinions of others. Others are more analytical and do not easily change their minds (Faber and O'Guinn 1992; Cole and Sherrell 1995).

Studies in psychology have proposed two different modes of processing information: the first is referred to as experiential or impulsive; the second as analytical-rational (Epstein *et al.* 1996). This explains the attitudinal ambivalence of the Chinese elite toward luxury goods, as we found in our in-depth interviews. For example, the impulsiveness displayed during the purchase of a luxury product, and the analytical thinking that the same individual may experience after purchase when he realizes that he possesses many similar products, may induce a feeling of dissonance and guilt.

Behavior and conscious thought are a joint function of the two systems, which engage in seamless, integrated interaction; but these systems are sometimes in conflict and the individual experiences a struggle between feeling and thought. These are the ubiquitous conflicts between heart and mind that can be observed in everyday life: "My reason told me to buy the Volkswagen, but my heart told me to buy the Stingray." The conflict between the rational (analytical) system and the experiential (impulsive) system presents a choice: ordinary brand or luxury brand.

Such ambivalent attitudes toward luxury goods and consumption exist in every society, irrespective of cultural background and social category, as researchers in emerging economies have found (see Dubois, Laurent, Czellar, 2000). However, consumers experience different degrees of ambivalence towards luxury goods and consumption depending on their social status and the cultural context.

Towards a consumer typology

Based on the three dimensions outlined above, we conducted a quantitative analysis of 312 individuals in four cities: Beijing, Shanghai, Guangzhou and Chengdu. The three dimensions divided the Chinese luxury market into four groups: luxury lovers, luxury followers, luxury intellectuals and luxury laggards (Table 3.2).

TABLE 3.2: *Typology of the Chinese luxury consumer*

	Dimension one: conspicuousness/ functionality	Dimension two: individualism/ collectivism	Dimension three: impulsive/analytical thinking
Luxury lovers	Conspicuousness	Collectivism	Analytical
Luxury followers	Conspicuousness	Collectivism	Impulsive
Luxury intellectuals	Functionality	Individualism	Analytical
Luxury laggards	Functionality	Individualism	Impulsive

Two matrices show how the four segments are positioned.

First matrix: Impulsive/analytical thinking process, and individualist/ collectivist dimensions

The luxury lovers and followers are both conspicuous and collectivist, conspicuousness and collectivism being related characteristics. But they differ in the analytical/impulsive dimension (see Figure 3.1 below).

The luxury lovers analyze the brand, and are not much influenced by others. They decide to buy because of the design, the color, and the model. The follower is more impulsive, and when the brand is well-known, he may seize an opportunity, either when there is a test, or trial, or price opportunity.

As for luxury laggards and luxury intellectuals, they are both individualist. But while the laggards are impulsive, the intellectuals are analytical. From the qualitative study it is clear that luxury

FIGURE 3.1: *The segmentation matrix I: Individualist and Impulsive dimensions*

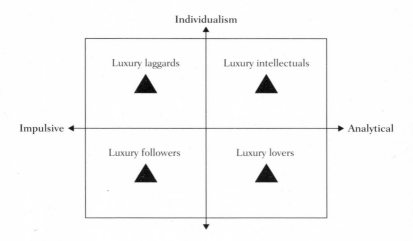

laggards are very clearly price-oriented. They buy luxury goods systematically during sales periods. This behavior explains why, in Matrix I, the result of the quantitative study shows that they are impulsive towards luxury goods. This is price-impulsiveness. Another indicator which can explain the impulsiveness of the laggards towards luxury buying is their income level, which was significantly lower than that of the other segments; which explains why they buy luxury goods only during sales or discount periods. When they find a good deal, they buy impulsively, without further thinking. Because the luxury lovers were found to have a significantly higher income level, they were less influenced by price considerations and were more analytical in their luxury purchases.

Second matrix: conspicuousness/functionality dimensions, and individualism/collectivism dimensions

In the second matrix (shown in Figure 3.2), the distribution of the four segments does not equilibrate across cells. There are two empty quadrants in the matrix. This means that there are very few Chinese

FIGURE 3.2: *The segmentation matrix II: Individualist and Conspicuous dimensions*

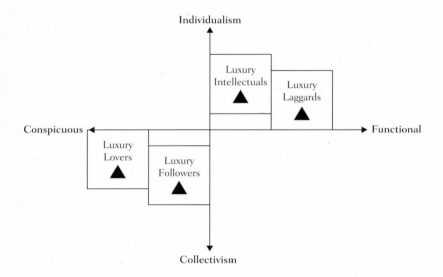

luxury consumers who have "conspicuous-individualist" and "functional-collectivist" profiles. The luxury intellectuals and the laggards are both located in the individualist and functional quadrant; the luxury lovers and the followers are located in the conspicuous and collectivist quadrant, although the degrees of conspicuousness and functionality of the four segments vary.

These results are very logical and in line with the motivations for buying luxury goods in Chinese society. Conspicuousness is linked with the social considerations of individuals; for example, to buy conspicuous luxury goods in order to demonstrate wealth and success to friends, colleagues and others. Thus, the conspicuous consumers are collectivist too.

And functional luxury consumers choose certain luxury goods in order to fulfill functional needs or their desire for possession. They often ignore the conspicuousness of the product, but focus on the excellent quality and sophisticated design. Thus, their choice has fewer social considerations, such as the desire to show off. They are consequently functional individualists.

The differences in segment distribution in the four principal cities or regions were significant: there were more luxury lovers and luxury followers in Guangzhou (50%) and in Shanghai (39.1%) than in Chengdu (36.6%) or Beijing (31.1%). The heaviest concentration of intellectuals was in Beijing (42.2%) while the heaviest concentration of laggards was in Chengdu (46.7%). Table 3.3 presents a breakdown of typical luxury consumers and the percentage of each group in each city.

TABLE 3.3: *Luxury consumers in the main Chinese cities*

	Beijing	Shanghai	Guangzhou	Chengdu
Luxury products customers	More traditional customers: diplomats, civil servants, managers in state companies, tourists and business customers	Modern international economic hub: business people, managers from the private sector, middle-upper and upper-middle class, tourists	Longstanding contacts with the Western world: international business people, from Middle East, Africa, South East Asia, America, Hong Kong, Taiwan, and so on	More recent contacts with the Western world: with customers mainly from middle-upper and upper-middle class from the industrial sector
Lovers	15.6%	13%	22.5%	3.3%
Followers	15.6%	26.1%	27.5%	33.3%
Intellectuals	42.2%	33.7%	30%	16.7%
Laggards	26.6%	27.2%	20%	46.7%
Modes of Communication	Sponsorship and events Business press Magazines Main appeals: Exclusiveness uniqueness elegance	Business press, posters Main appeals: Modernity Success	Business, commercial and popular culture Television Close to Hong Kong communication channels Main appeal: Fashion	Local newspapers Posters Main appeal: Success and social belonging

Managerial implications of attitudes and behavior

In addition, the group differences in innovativeness, brand loyalty and post-purchase guilt also confirm the significance of the cluster results.

Innovativeness

In previous marketing research, innovativeness was particularly relevant to technological products (such as home electronic products), where some models offer an abundance of features and functions, while others propose just a minimum of essential features or functions (Schiffman and Kanuk 2000).

According to Schütte and Ciarlante (1998), and in accordance with traditional diffusion theory, consumers are categorized according to when they adopt a new product. The five most frequently quoted adopter categories are: innovators, early adopters, early majority, late majority and laggards. In a Western context, these categories are generally depicted as a normal distribution curve with innovators, early adopters and laggards accounting for 2.5%, 13.5% and 16%, respectively (Rogers 1962; Kotler 1996) and very specific strategies should be designed for each category (Le Nagard-Assayag and Pras 2003). The early and late majorities each account for 34% of the total population ultimately adopting a product. However, in an Asian cultural context, very few Asian consumers are prepared to take the social risk of being innovators and trying a new product first. The discomfort of being left behind, however, induces them to follow others who have tried it. Trials by early buyers thus soften the perceived risk for followers, who are then inclined to "pile in" in their haste to buy. This forms the two tails of the distribution curve—much lower among Asian consumers—resulting in a steeper distribution curve, as shown in Figure 3.3. In addition, the left tail is longer, reflecting a hesitation to try the new product,

FIGURE 3.3: *Diffusion of a new luxury product in an Asian context*

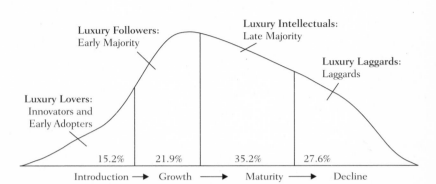

whereas the right tail of the curve drops off sharply as consumers are ready to switch brands once the normative standards of their reference group change. The Schütte and Ciarlante study pointed out that no published data existed up to that point (and there has been none since) to prove the validity of a shorter and biased diffusion curve.

Innovativeness and brand loyalty

There is actually an inverse correlation between the innovativeness of luxury products and luxury brand loyalty. The more sensitive consumers are to the innovations of luxury products, the lower their brand loyalty will be. This link has some important implications for the luxury industry, since most of the luxury brands have legendary creations with a long history behind them. The classic models of each luxury firm are a precious heritage and the core value of the brand, such as the perfume Chanel No. 5 and the monogram design of Louis Vuitton's leather goods. For consumers with a higher response to innovativeness, such as the luxury lovers, the traditional models and products of the most prestigious luxury firms may not be the most attractive. Thus, the pursuit of innovativeness and new creation exceeds the power of the brand and becomes the priority for the lovers in choosing their luxury products.

However, for the luxury intellectuals and the laggards, classic models and products are more attractive than new models, because they focus more on the functionality of the product and on the value of the brand. Traditional luxury consumers love the classic models and trust the brands—which explains their higher brand loyalty.

Traditional luxury firms, while maintaining the loyalty of traditional luxury consumers, work on creating new models, enlarging their product categories and using new materials to attract more lovers and followers and to give greater choice to the intellectuals and the laggards. However, for new luxury firms, innovativeness is the main and only point that attracts their clients, most of whom are luxury lovers or luxury followers. If the newcomers want to stay in the luxury industry, they cannot afford to rely solely on lovers and followers as clients, because the consumers in these two segments are prone to switching to other brands at any time. Thus, new luxury brands need to keep their successful models and create their own legends in order to attract traditional luxury consumers: the intellectuals and the laggards. Thus, a real luxury brand will have consumers from all four segments, enabling luxury clients with different motivations to find what they want under the same brand.

Brand loyalty

Research suggests that brand loyalty is correlated with the consumer's degree of involvement: high involvement leads to an extensive search for information and, ultimately, to brand loyalty, while low involvement leads to exposure and brand awareness, and then possibly to brand habit (see Schiffman and Kanuk 2000). As a customer's satisfaction with a product increases along with repeated purchases, the search for information about alternative brands decreases. Evidence suggests that loyal consumers—those who have a strong commitment to a brand, service, or retail store—show strong resistance to attempts at counter-persuasion. Brand loyalty among the four segments increases in the following order: luxury lovers, luxury followers, luxury intellectuals and luxury laggards.

Post-purchase guilt

What makes post-purchase dissonance relevant to marketing strategists is the premise that dissonance propels consumers to reduce the unpleasant feelings created by rival thoughts. A variety of tactics are open to consumers to reduce post-purchase dissonance. The consumer can rationalize the decision as being wise, seek out advertisements that support the choice (while avoiding dissonance-creating competitive ads), try to "sell" to friends the positive features of the brand, or look to known satisfied consumers for reassurance (Schiffman and Kanuk 2000).

Marketers, too, can help reduce any post-purchase uncertainty by including messages in their advertising specifically aimed at reinforcing consumers' decisions by "complimenting their wisdom," offering stronger guarantees or warranties, increasing the number and efficiency of its services, or providing detailed brochures on how to use its products correctly. In addition, marketers are increasingly developing affinity or relationship programs designed to reward good customers and to build customer loyalty and satisfaction. As noted earlier, the luxury brand companies should also develop programs similar to those employed by service-intensive industries, such as airlines, hotel chains, and major car-rental companies (Schiffman and Kanuk 2000).

For Chinese luxury consumers, post-purchase guilt is one of the most significant obstacles to consuming luxury products. The psychological dissonance and inconsistency with their traditional values make them feel uneasy about deciding to buy and consume luxury goods. As noted earlier, post-purchase guilt decreases the rate of repeat purchases and thus reduces brand loyalty.

Among the four segments, the followers suffer the most from post-purchase guilt. The intellectuals and laggards show little or no guilt but they do not demonstrate strong brand loyalty through repeat purchases. The brand loyalty of the followers is lower than even that of intellectuals and laggards. They want to be trendy and therefore buy the most popular models and products of the season (following the lovers). However, these products soon become unfashionable and their feelings of guilt come from having spent a great deal of money in order to be trendy. At the same time, they cannot resist the temptation to buy the new season's products. For the followers, post-purchase guilt accompanies every luxury purchase.

On the other hand, the much weaker post-purchase guilt experienced by the intellectuals is on a psychological level and arises from a conflict between traditional Chinese consumption values and their personal involvement in luxury goods.

The implications of these findings for luxury firms are clear: decrease the post-purchase guilt of the followers and increase post-purchase reassurance for the intellectuals and laggards. For the former, the most efficient way may be to change their choice of products, offering them more classic models, which allow trendy people to feel neither unfashionable nor too fashionable. This may have the effect of decreasing the risk of feeling unfashionable while increasing confidence of being trendy. This could also result in increasing their purchases of classic models and, in turn, their brand loyalty.

For the intellectuals and laggards, luxury companies could add services to make them feel as comfortable as possible with their purchase. These services will vary according to the luxury company and the products on offer but may include such things as personalizing the purchased item (even if it was bought on promotion), a loyal client club, and so on.

Conclusion

The rapid and continuing economic development and social evolution in mainland China will see corresponding changes in Chinese luxury-consumer behavior. The size and balance within and between consumer groups will evolve, with increasing numbers of lovers and followers emerging as the younger generations with their more hedonist lifestyles join the throng of luxury consumers. As this happens, post-purchase guilt will decrease. On the other hand, however, many of the traditions and festivals lost following the Cultural Revolution are now being revived, with the Chongyang,[8] Duanwu[9] and Qingming[10] festivals recently being declared national holidays. Such traditional values, which are a strong component of the Chinese identity, will continue to influence people and help ensure that the four groups of luxury consumers in China will continue to exist for a long time to come.

ENDNOTES

1   This chapter was jointly written with Bernard Pras, Professor of Marketing in Essec and University of Dauphine, Paris.

2   For a full account of this phenomenon, see Thorstein *The Theory of the Leisure Class* (1899).

3   In 2004, the U.N. criterion for middle-class status was US$6,000 per capita per year (RMB5,000 per month). In China the annual middle-class family income standard ranges from US$7,264 to US$60,532 (RMB60,000 to RMB500,000—National Statistics Bureau in Beijing, 2005).

4   The average annual per-capita income in China in 2008 was RMB15,781(US$2,320) (State Statistical Bureau, 2009); the national GDP was around US$3,100 per capita.

5   In accordance with Deng's opening up and reform policy since 1978.

6   From Duke Zhuang in *Zuo Zhuan*, the first Chinese chronological history, recording events during the Spring and Autumn period (770–476 B.C.) of China's history.

7   Si-ma Guang (A.D. 1019–86) of the Song Dynasty (A.D. 960–1279).

8   Held on the ninth day of the ninth lunar month, Chongyang Festival is also called "Double Ninth Festival." In Chinese, nine is regarded as the number of Yang (the masculine principle, as opposed to Yin, which is feminine). The ninth day of the ninth month has two Yang numbers, and "chong" in Chinese means "double"—hence, Chongyang. During this autumn festival, people eat Chongyang cake, climb mountains and pay homage to chrysanthemums by drinking chrysanthemum wine.

9   Duanwu, The Dragon Boat Festival, has the longest history of all Chinese festivals. Held during the summer months, it celebrates the dragon boats

which attempted to rescue Chu Yuan, a patriotic poet, who drowned him-
self (277 B.C.) because his king would not listen to his advice. The king's
failure to heed this advice led to the kingdom being conquered. People eat
tzungtzu and rice, which was the food used to try to revive Chu Yuan.

10 Qingming, in which people honor and pay respect to the ancestors, has taken
place in early April since 732 A.D. During the festival, people visit the graves of
departed ones and also celebrate the departure of winter and the coming
of the springtime (踏青, "treading on the greenery").

Rolex in China[1]

According to the statistics of the Federation of the Swiss Watch Industry (FH), in 2008 the industry recorded exports equivalent to US$15 billion, an increase of almost US$1 billion. As shown in Table 1, while Hong Kong was the leading destination, mainland China recorded a 43.1% increase over the previous year, to be ranked seventh in the overall standings. This reflected a huge and growing demand for imported watches in the Chinese market. Asia was therefore the

TABLE 1: *World distribution of Swiss watch exports, 2008*

	Country or Region	Values (US$)	Change 2008/2007
1	Hong Kong	2.51 billion	+10.9%
2	United States	2.23 billion	− 3%
3	Japan	1.12 billion	− 4.5%
4	France	1.03 billion	+15.1%
5	Italy	0.98 billion	+2.5%
6	Germany	852 million	+10.2%
7	China (Mainland)	770 million	+43.1%
8	Singapore	730 million	+16.8%
9	United Arab Emirates	628 million	+27.6%
10	Britain	598 million	− 2.7%

Source: Federation of Swiss Watch Industry 2008

main source of growth (+13.2%) for the industry, well ahead of Europe, which recorded a general slowdown in pace, ending the year at +3.6%.

As shown in Table 2 below, within China, Rolex claimed 7.11% of watch sales in 2007, considerably behind market leader Omega (22.75%), Rado (8.19%), and Longines (7.62%), which all belong to the Swatch Group. The table does not include jewelry makers such as Cartier or Bulgari which also sell watches. The international brands also face competition from local watch brands such as Rossini, Fiyta (the official watch supplier for Chinese astronauts), Tianwang and Ebohr.

In April 2009, Touch media in Shanghai, conducted a survey of Chinese preferences for watches. Of the 180,000 respondents, 31.7% preferred Swiss-made prestigious watches, while 27.1% preferred those made by fashion brands. Given a choice, 22.3% said they preferred a classic watch, while 18.9% opted for a modern cool-function watch. Of the respondents, 28.1% didn't own a

TABLE 2: *Watch sales in China, 2007*

Retail Amount Ranking	Brands	Market Share (retail amount) %	Market Share (retail quantity) %	Retail Quantity Ranking
1	Omega	22.75	1.94	12
2	Rado	8.19	1.06	17
3	Longines	7.62	2.30	10
4	Rolex	7.11	0.25	49
5	Tissot	4.96	4.11	8
6	Tudor	4.71	0.57	30
7	Titoni	4.29	1.88	14
8	Rossini (Chinese)	2.93	9.61	1
9	Citizen	2.83	6.01	5
10	Enicar	2.79	2.20	11
11	Fiyta (Chinese)	2.67	5.50	6
12	Tianwang (Chinese)	2.59	7.25	3
13	Ebohr (Chinese)	2.58	8.23	2
14	Casio	1.66	6.29	4
15	Ernest Borel	1.47	0.97	19

Source: Annual Book of China Watch Market 2007

watch; 32.6% had one, 30% had between two to five watches, and 9.3% had more than five watches. Almost half (49.3%) said they would not buy a Chinese-made watch.

A brief history of Rolex

The company that eventually became Rolex as we know it today was founded by a German national, Hans Wilhelm Wilsdorf, and a British native, Alfred James Davis, in 1905. Their company was registered as "Rolex" in Switzerland in 1908 and in London in 1912. The name "Rolex" was chosen because it was clear, easy to spell, and easy to pronounce.

Rolex has a very particular status. It belongs to the Wilsdorf trust and therefore cannot be sold to any interested international group and is not subject to the usual shareholder pressure to produce short-term benefits in the form of dividends. As a result, it is able to reinvest profits to improve distribution and after-sales services and to increase research and development. Rolex is one of the few big players that do not follow a multi-brand strategy. The company is extremely secretive and all the numbers presented in this case study are our own estimates.

Rolex employs about 6,000 people worldwide, the majority of whom (3,300) are based in Geneva. It sells around 750,000 watches each year, with an estimated turnover of between US$2.2–2.8 billion. The company has 22 subsidiaries around the world.

Marketing strategies

Conservatism and tradition are the credos of the Rolex strategy: it has sold the same product and used the same communication strategy for many decades.

The communication strategy features two distinctive points: the use of sponsorship and, particularly, celebrity endorsement; and the emphasis on being a mysterious brand.

The use of testimonials has always played a key role in the company's communication strategy since the first advertisement in 1927 and Rolex has always been faithful to this concept. Rolex tries to exalt individual success, choosing strong personalities from a range of disciplines—opera singers Placido Domingo and Cecilia Bartoli, dancer Yuanyuan Tan, cellist Yoyo Ma, equestrian-eventers Meredith Michaels-Beerbaum, Rodrigo Pessoa and Zara Philips, golfers Lorena Ochoa and Phil Mickelson, explorers David Doubilet, Rune Gjeldnes, Alain Hubert and Jean Troillet, tennis players Roger Federer and Ana Ivanovic. The idea is to choose people who have made significant achievements in their respective fields and will become part of history, so that Rolex can join them in writing it.

The "Rolex" brand name is already so famous that it can concentrate on fully expressing and developing the brand identity. Perfectly in line with the idea of a long-term strategy, Rolex uses a selective marketing strategy with a view to targeting the desired customer very directly. Choosing ambassadors is not an easy task but Rolex has developed a talent for discovering future champions. It seeks out young talent and accompanies them until they become great champions, a strategy that has since been adopted by rivals such as Tag Heuer and Omega.

In choosing ambassadors who are recognized for their achievements, Rolex has become the incarnation of success, accomplishment and extending individual horizons. It is definitely the watch people buy when they have achieved something in their life. The design of the watch is such that it is instantly recognizable in its own right and anyone wearing it is clearly identified with achievement through hard work, talent, passion, tenacity and courage. However, the downside is that it is not beyond the grasp of the nouveau riche and their flashy associations with easy money. Being taken up in this way by people seeking to display and prove their success has, through no fault of its own, tarnished the Rolex image somewhat.

According to Kevin Roberts, CEO of Saatchi & Saatchi: "Mystery opens up emotion. It lies in the stories, metaphors, and iconic characters that give a relationship its texture. Mystery is a key part of creating loyalty beyond reason." It combines the past, the present and the future, tapping into dreams and inspiring through the myths and icons it creates. This is true of Rolex, which is certainly the most mysterious brand in the watch-making world, not only because of its particular status and the secrecy surrounding its financial performance but also thanks to some key points of its communication strategy.

The principle of introducing the units little by little in a given market is known as the "rarity principle,"[2] which works on the basis that "luxury brands must be desired by all, [but] consumed only by the happy few."[3]

Rolex in China

Having a strong financial background enabled Rolex to expand quickly in the Chinese market. It entered the mainland market in 1995 in cooperation with Peace Mark, the largest watch retailer in Asia. It created subsidiaries in Beijing, Shanghai and Guangzhou and also entered 12 secondary cities, including Shenyang, Tianjin, Hangzhou, and Chongqing. At the beginning of 2009 it had 27 official mono-brand stores (although these actually sell Tudor, Rolex's lower-price brand, as well).

As elsewhere in the world, Rolex's marketing activities focus on advertising and sports events, using international celebrities. Since 2007, Rolex has been the official sponsor for the China Tennis Open in Beijing, and in 2008 it replaced Rado and Longines as the official time-keeper for the Tennis Masters Cup in Shanghai.

The company's image in China is quite different from that which it enjoys elsewhere in the world. The Rolex brand became a symbol of success during the early years of Deng's reforms in the 1980s when it spread from Hong Kong to Guangdong. But along the way, it has become distorted by being strongly associated with the conspicuous consumption and flashy lifestyles of China's newly rich. Now, it is associated with arrogance.

Because the brand is associated with the first generation of rich-but-rude Cantonese factory owners, younger Chinese view the brand differently. In maintaining its traditional values and image, the company runs the risk of being perceived as aging and out of touch. This strong reliance on tradition can also be perceived as a lack of ideas and innovation. To win back more-youthful consumers, it may be necessary to emphasize intergenerational influences, "the within-family transmission of information, beliefs and resources from one generation to the next,"[4] as captured in Patek Philippe's slogan: "You actually never own a Patek Philippe. You merely take care of it for the next generation."

Recognizing the huge potential offered by the China market, Rolex keeps investing in this region. However, it is among the most commonly counterfeited brands and is often sold illegally on the street and on the internet. These fakes are mainly produced in China because of the ease in copying the general design, and retail for anything from US$5 to US$1,000 for high-end replicas in solid gold. By some accounts, over 75% of all replica watches produced annually are copies of Rolex Oyster Perpetual designs. Fake Rolexes are among the top 10 items promoted via e-mail spam.

Major issues

The number-one issue with the competitive standing of the brand is at the worldwide level, where the Rolex group is considered to be roughly equivalent to the Swatch luxury brand division and the Richemont Cartier groups (Rolex and Swatch having approximately 25% and Richemont Cartier around 20–22% of the worldwide luxury watch market).

Although Rolex has a considerable presence in China, it is still a long way behind the Swatch group and other brands, as we saw earlier. Is the issue here that Rolex came too late to the market? Maybe the recent move toward sponsoring tennis activities and establishing a higher visibility is a move in the right direction. But is this enough? Perhaps it needs to localize its international image a little more by appropriating famous Chinese faces in its marketing and communication activities.

Another issue concerns the respective sizes of the Rolex and Tudor brands. At the worldwide level, for every two or three Tudor watches sold, there are 10 Rolex purchases. In China, however, more people purchase Tudor watches. Is this a question of pricing strategy or other issues? At this stage, there are two possible explanations: either, the Rolex Company has had a very special brand strategy and has decided to push Tudor very strongly in a first stage; or there really is a negative attitude toward the Rolex brand, which explains why Chinese people seem to be scaling down to Tudor. The problem is that, in some ways, Tudor is perfect for Chinese consumers: they spend much less money but have a Swiss-made watch from the Rolex tradition. The price-value ratio of the Rolex brand is not strong enough at present to encourage people to make that extra investment when there are so many aggressive alternatives in the Chinese market.

This leads obviously to the last issue: Is there a strong negative attitude about the Rolex brand in China and is its association with the image of the "rude Cantonese boss" so strongly perceived that the brand has lost some of its attractiveness for the sophisticated and wealthy central or northern Chinese customers? If so, it would then be a question of determining the kind of marketing activities that could modify this position over time.

What other marketing and communication activities could the company conduct within its overall worldwide framework? At present, Rolex's marketing and communication activities in China are too reserved, not bold enough, for this market, which makes it seem as if the brand lacks confidence in itself. Its core values, such as success and achievement, are the dominant values of the China market and should be perfect for advertising itself. Strengthening these core symbolic values will be the key to its success over the next 10 years, especially during and after the current financial crisis. China's economic and geopolitical position in the world is shifting, and the Chinese will have more modern values as a result. These new values are likely to veer away from those of the flashy Cantonese bosses, and resonate with Rolex's core values. Hence, the key to Rolex's success over the next 10 years may well be to communicate its values more boldly.

ENDNOTES

1   This case is intended for educational use and as a basis for discussion, and does not represent a model for handling any managerial situation. The case was compiled from public and online sources.

2   Dubois and Paternault 1985, "Observations: understanding the world of international luxury brands," *Journal of Advertising Research* 35 (4): 69–76.

3   Kapferer, 1996 "Managing Luxury Brands," *Journal of Brand Management,* 4 (4): 251–60.

4   Moore, Wilkie and Lutz 2002, "Passing the torch: intergenerational influences as a source of brand equity," *Journal of Marketing* 66 (2): 17–37.

CHAPTER 4

How to Distribute in China

I N ANY MARKET, there are different ways of setting up luxury activities. But what makes China a slightly more difficult proposition is its size, its complexity and its marked regional differences. Unlike the United States, where some people start operating from California and others open their first activity on the East Coast, the choice in China is to start from Guangzhou, Shanghai or Beijing; three possible entry-points whose financial requirements, personal demands and long-term potential make them entirely different entities. Also, the temptation to start everywhere at once is not a viable alternative in a country where 45 cities have between a million and five million inhabitants and 12 have more than five million.

To begin this chapter, we describe the different systems available to start operations in China. We then indicate the major economic and legal aspects of the different alternatives, before identifying major potential partners to study prior to moving into China.

Operational Framework

While a wholly owned subsidiary is the first thought that crosses the minds of many when asked how best to start operations in China, other approaches are possible.

Direct imports

In the United States or Japan, the first entry point into the country for many brand owners is to let major department stores acquire and distribute the brand, often on an exclusive basis. For example, a new fashion or watch brand may decide that the best course is to allow the brand to be sold exclusively at Nieman Marcus department stores in the United States or at Takashimaya stores in Japan. This system has the advantage of being cheap, secure and easy. As a first step, it is possible to see if the brand finds its own consumer base, and to wait a few years to see how things develop.

In China, almost no department-store company is strong enough to provide this kind of service to a foreign brand. Of these stores, Parkson is probably one of the strongest. Founded in Malaysia in 1987, the group came to China in 1994 and had 28 department stores in the country in 2008, including two in Beijing and two in Shanghai. The rest are in cities such as Anshan, Changsha, Chengdu, Chongqing, Dalian, Guiyang and Harbin, among others. In its home market, Parkson has two different types of stores: some very upscale; others more middle market. In China, it has positioned itself as middle/middle-upper market. It has strong brand recognition among Chinese customers and focuses on fashion and lifestyle, providing a wide range of merchandise. While it is quite important for perfumes and cosmetics, its positioning in fashion does not necessarily suggest it as the ideal entry for a very upscale brand.

Only Isetan, the Japanese department store, can perhaps bring this top image. However, even this is marginal because it has only five stores—Shanghai Mei Long Zhen, Shanghai Huating, Tianjin, Shenyang and Chengdu—and has no presence at all in Beijing.

Other Japanese department stores have an even more limited presence: Seibu has three stores in Hong Kong, but only two in mainland China: Chengdu and Shengyang. Sogo has two stores in China.

The Hong Kong chain Lane Crawford had six stores in Hong Kong and two in mainland China in 2008: one in Beijing and one in Shanghai.

A local operation of a similar type to these three foreign competitors is Maison Mode. Despite the implications of its name, the group—created in Shanghai in 1994—deals in upscale men's and women's fashion, carrying strong brands such as Gucci and

Salvatore Ferragamo. It has five stores: Shanghai, Beijing, Chengdu, Chongqing and Xi'an.

Also worth mentioning is Guangzhou Friendship Stores, with three locations in Guangzhou, one in Shanghai and another in Dalian. Prior to the Communist era, there were many more department stores but they closed down or left the country to develop their business in Hong Kong. Some have returned since but many never came back.

Other operators include Wangfujing (with locations in Beijing and Chengdu and New World department store).

The Beijing Hualian Group is a leading Chinese retailer which recently acquired the Seiyu Group's three department stores in Singapore and renamed them BHG. The group's main activities include the operation of supermarkets and department stores, as well as the sale of general merchandise, textiles, daily-use products and fresh fruits and vegetables. Hualian Group and the Taiwanese retailer Shin Kong Place jointly opened a new department store in Beijing West CBD, which has become the new landmark of high-end and luxury brand malls.

Beijing's INTIME group is a Hong Kong-listed department-store chain which started as a retailing and real estate business in Zhejiang Province, one of the country's wealthiest provinces, where it currently owns five department stores.

Because Chinese department stores are not yet international, in that their merchandisers and buyers are not visiting Paris or Milan on a systematic basis to buy fashion, any negotiations will have to take place in China.

There are other department stores in China but these tend to have limited outlets and operate in a very traditional way. Although the large luxury shopping centers that have been developed in various cities are financed from Hong Kong, Taiwan and Singapore, these groups act only as property developers and leasers: they never purchase merchandise.

Overall, then, the department stores cannot really provide a strong, nationwide distribution network.

Importer-distributors

The most common system is to use an importer-distributor who purchases the goods in Europe and assumes responsibility for promoting the brand in China, visiting the different sales outlets to promote the merchandise.

The initial move into China was led by Hong Kong-based distributors such as Dickson Concepts, Bluebell and, to a lesser extent, Melee. Having established long-standing relationships of trust with a "principal" in Europe or the United States in distributing merchandise in Hong Kong or Taiwan, they were able to obtain exclusive distribution rights to sell that brand to department stores or local retailers in China. They now have a strong set-up in China, generally with an official commercial license to operate and a marketing office in Shanghai. For a European fashion brand or a perfume company, this was a very secure way to enter the Chinese market.

However, in the second stage of developing the Chinese market, direct contact with a distributor in, say, Shanghai seemed a much better way to operate and today the business focus is slowly moving away from Hong Kong, Singapore and Taipei towards places such as Shanghai, Beijing and Shenzhen.

In this case, the distributor purchases the products abroad under contract and pays the necessary import duties and other costs. He then organizes the logistics and deliveries, sets up the necessary financial arrangements, and organizes the sales.

For simplicity's sake, the importer-distributor also assumes responsibility for the advertising and promotional budget in China. There is usually a contractual obligation to spend a percentage of wholesale sales on advertising, under the supervision of the brand owner. Generally, importer-distributors may be tempted to spend some of their advertising budgets in sales-related activities, as this makes their life easier when they visit retailers and try to sell the brand. But life is not that simple, because it is much more complicated and time-consuming to run a large number of individualized promotional and public relations activities than to place an order for a large media campaign with an advertising agency. The principals, on the other hand, have a strong preference for media advertising because their priority is to develop greater awareness and psychological responsiveness to their brand.

Subsidiaries

Of course, setting up a subsidiary is a sure way to get started in China. Unlike many other places in the world, it is quite easy to start and register a corporation in China, even if it is a wholly foreign-owned firm. The necessary license of operation is generally easy to obtain.

Choice of location is, of course, very important and opinions vary on the best place to be. Shanghai is a very strong retail center on the east coast and has easy access to the 10 major cities. Some people clearly prefer Beijing, finding it cheaper and more effective. Others think that Guangzhou has advantages, being close to Hong Kong.

Joint ventures

While similar to subsidiaries in some ways, joint ventures provide a set up which has some added flexibility.

For the first foreign brands entering China there was no alternative but to be an "outside principal" and a minority joint-venture partner, usually with a state-owned and sometimes state-run distribution company. It made sense for the foreign firm to start a joint venture and reach an agreement with the new owner as a way to guarantee the brand's development. However, as the market opened and China entered the World Trade Organization, many of these companies slowly became private and the foreign partners have become majority shareholders.

Joint ventures are an easier means of entry than a wholly-owned subsidiary. The Chinese joint-venture partner would invest its own money in the company and could provide a direct understanding of the local language, culture and business traditions. It also facilitated all the administrative procedures.

Which of these alternatives proves to be the most effective entry path for a particular luxury brand will depend on the investment it is prepared to make in the Chinese market and, more importantly, on the amount of time its executives are ready to spend in visiting and getting to know the market. Without this, there can be no real understanding of the specific conditions that prevail or of the necessary adjustments that must be made in adapting their product offerings to the particular needs of the market.

There is one system which definitely does not work, although it is frequently used. This is the case where a foreign group purchases a majority interest in a local Chinese company (anything from 51% to 75%, say) and leaves the former owner to run the company. The majority owners must be sure they have executives who accept and understand the basic philosophy of the group. Management control and accountabilities must be clearly stated. This cannot be over-stated. In our experience, this is often neglected, perhaps because of language difficulties or cultural differences.

Business analysis

To compare the validity of a distributor's set-up to that of a subsidiary, it is necessary to look at the costs and normal conditions of their respective operations.

A distributor may purchase brand merchandise and pay for it within, say, 60 or 90 days. In the case of a subsidiary, the yearly cost includes the rental cost of an office in, say, the center of Shanghai, and of a warehouse. Then there are staff costs, which vary but can, if we incorporate a general manager, a chief financial officer, a marketing manager and immediate support staff, reach US$1–2 million. The purchase of the inventory is another added cash drain. Here again, critical mass is a very important element.

As a rule of thumb, it does not make sense to start a subsidiary on anything less than wholesale sales of US$5 million.

Major Chinese partners

The choice available to a principal looking for a distributor in China is between a Hong Kong-based company which is well organized, knows how to distribute an international brand and is used to reporting but which does not necessarily have a China-wide capability and concentrates on the major Eastern cities; and a Chinese distributor, which may be not so well organized but is used to dealing with Chinese customers and administration. The Chinese distributor may have either a national focus or a regional focus, the latter being another drawback.

Below, we present the major distributors, starting with those based in Hong Kong and Singapore before moving to those on the mainland.

Major Hong Kong/Singapore distributors

Bluebell is probably the best-known Asian distributor. Established by a French family in 1954, it started out selling perfumes but has since moved into luxury lifestyle businesses. These include Davidoff cigars and accessories and, primarily, fashion brands including Blumarine, Moschino, Paul Smith, Jimmy Choo, J.M. Weston among others.

In 2008 Bluebell had 2,400 employees and operated 500 points of sale in Asia, generally as mono-brand stores dedicated to the brands for which they have exclusive distribution contracts. Of these, only eight stores were in mainland China (compared, for example, to 24 in Taiwan and 59 in Hong Kong) with their strongest brands: Blumarine, Paul Smith and Moschino.

In February 2007, the *International Herald Tribune* reported comments made by Bluebell's Chief Executive Officer Eric Douilhet who, in a speech to the Hong Kong Chamber of Commerce in October 2006, gave a clear indication that its Chinese activities were still unprofitable: "I was definitely expecting sales to be higher, the losses to be smaller," he said. "If the time comes that we realize the money we spend is more than we earn, then obviously we will reconsider our presence." From this we can safely infer that Bluebell is not ready to invest massively in China or to make any major new investments. In fact, it may retire completely to its main bases in Japan, Korea and Hong Kong, retaining only its network of franchised cigar stores, and a joint venture to operate furniture stores with Roset, HC 28 and Hugues Chevalier.

Former Hong Kong watch manufacturer **Dickson Concepts** has become a major luxury distributor, with 500 shops and total sales around US$400 million. Its presence in mainland China is quite strong, with 228 stores, compared to only 68 in Hong Kong and 170 in Taiwan. The geographical set-up is quite different from that of Bluebell, as it does not operate in Korea or Japan.

The main brands it distributes are Tommy Hilfiger, Chopard, Goyard, Bertolucci and Royal Diamond. But in some of its shopping arcades (the Jin Jian Shopping Center in Shanghai, for example) it also rents out stores for Gucci, Chloe and Bottega Veneta.

All mainland Chinese activities are run from Hong Kong, but there is an office in Shanghai. In mainland China alone, the Group operates 51 Tommy Hilfiger shops. The Group is also the controlling investor in the Harvey Nichols department store in London and the French luxury house S.G. Dupont. Dickson Poon is also the franchised operator of three SEIBU department stores in Hong Kong and two in mainland China (Chengdu and Shenyang).

Eternal was established in 1980 by Steven Lau. It is an agent for brands of perfumery and optical products. It started in Hong Kong, where some of its exclusive brands are present in 70% of the perfume shops. It then moved to Macau and to mainland China. In China, it is distributing products in 240 perfume shops and at 80 points of sale for optical frames. It represents the perfume brands Paco Rabanne, Nina Ricci, Burberry, Lanvin, Loewe, Lacoste, Carolina Herrera, Prada and many others. In the skin-care sector, it is the agent for Academic, Payot, Gatineau and Nickel. In the optical-frame segment, it is the exclusive distributor of Alfred Dunhill, Ferrari, Roberto Cavalli, Tag Heuer, Tom Ford, and Timberland products, among many others.

Fairton International Group was created in 1955 and became the Hong Kong and mainland China distributor for Bally in 1979.

HOW TO DISTRIBUTE IN CHINA   93

It assumed distribution for Max Mara, in 1987 and since then has acquired the distribution rights for Jean-Paul Gaultier, Kookai and Marina Rinaldi products.

Today, the Group operates 200 stores, including 51 in Hong Kong and 123 in mainland China. In China, major brands distributed are Max Mara (35 points of sale), Bally (31) and Kookai (27). It is also quite strong in Taiwan.

Hembly is an interesting case. Established in 2000 and listed on the Hong Kong stock market in 2006, it was created to provide supply-chain services to international apparel and accessories brands, including Armani, Benetton and Sisley. It has since become the owner of brands such as Sergio Tacchini and Gaetano Navarra, and the mainland Chinese distributor for Moschino. With sales exceeding US$50 million, it is currently in negotiations to acquire an important share of Italian fashion-manufacturing holding group Itiere.

Imaginex was created in 1992 by Peter Woo and is one of the strongest of the Hong Kong-based distributors. In mainland China, it operates in 43 cities and represents 22 international brands, including Agnès B, BCBG Max Azria, Hugo Boss, Dolce & Gabbana, DKNY, Galliano, Marc Jacob, Salvatore Ferragamo and Versace. It also distributes cosmetic products for the likes of Elizabeth Arden through wholesale channels.

It has 360 points of sale in mainland China, including several in major cities: 12 in Beijing, eight in Chengdu, and six in each of Shanghai, Guangzhou and Xi'an. In addition to its headquarters in Hong Kong, it has regional offices in Shanghai, Beijing and Taiwan. The company claims to make more profit from its Hong Kong operations than from the mainland.

Joyce Boutique Holdings is another of the major Hong Kong fashion distributors doing big things in China. The company, created by Joyce Ma, has its headquarters in Hong Kong, where it is listed on the Hong Kong Stock Exchange. It is also now incorporated in Bermuda and has sales of US$120 million. The group has 66 points of sale in mainland China: four large multi-label Joyce stores, 47 brand designer boutiques, 10 maxi shops and five beauty shops. The group has an operating profit of US$6.5 million and

94LUXURY CHINA

has known difficult times, with the resignation of the founder and her two daughters, Adrienne and Yvette, in March 2008.

Li & Fung Limited started in 2002 as the mainland China distributor for Calvin Klein Jeans. It has 85 outlets in China and is in most major department stores in Shanghai and Beijing, where it occupies clearly identified positions or shop-in-shops. It also distributes Calvin Klein underwear from 75 outlets in China.

Its other brands include Gant (acquired in 2005 and for which it has eight outlets, including a flagship store in Beijing) and Mango (acquired in 2003 and for which it handles 43 points of sale). Mango's retail value in mainland China is estimated at US$4 million.

The **Melee Group** was established in November 1994 by Chantana Ping Chan. Though based in Hong Kong, its legal address is in the British Virgin Islands. With more than 900 employees, it operates in China, Hong Kong and Taiwan as a distributor of perfumes and cosmetics and also manages its own beauty parlors in China. Subsidiaries include Far East Beauty Products Limited and Palaispa Beauty World in China, Franco Mercantile Agency Limited in Hong Kong and Wealth March Company Limited in Taiwan.

In China, the group distributes perfumes and cosmetics to more than 500 points of sale. Its Chinese head office is located in Shanghai, with a branch office in Beijing and sales offices in Chengdu, Tianjin, Chongqing and Guangzhou. It distributes Givenchy, Kenzo, Gucci, Dolce & Gabbana and Moschino perfumes, and Make Up For Ever cosmetics, among many other brands.

Its other distribution channels include two major chains (1000 Colors and Fiona Cosmetics), and independent perfumeries.

It also operates 22 Institutes in China, with exclusive use of Ericson Laboratoire, Mary Cohr and Thalgo professional products.

Shenzhen World Link Industry acts as a distributor in mainland China for Lanvin (three stores: Guangzhou, Beijing and Shanghai) and as a franchisee for Lacoste (11 stores in Beijing, Guangzhou and Qingdao). The company also has offices in Shenzhen and Beijing.

In summary, these eight large Hong Kong distributors operate more than 1,500 luxury points of sale in mainland China. Whether they are all profitable is not clear. Seven of them are undoubtedly powerful, well organized, used to reporting in a systematic way, accustomed to dealing with top luxury brands in China and able to find attractive store locations for a new brand. Any manager of a European luxury brand looking to find a distribution solution in China is well advised to start with those potential partners in Hong Kong.

Mainland Chinese distributors[1]

The following distributors are smaller than the Hong Kong or Singapore distributors listed above. Some work for a single brand and some also operate under license for some international brands.

Set up in Beijing in 1997, **Asian Development Enterprise** is the leading distributor of fragrances and cosmetics, with more than 1,000 employees in 30 major Chinese cities. Its perfumes include Hugo Boss, Bulgari, Davidoff, Salvatore Ferragamo, Vera Wang, Tous, and Calvin Klein. In the skincare business, it distributes Global suncare, Lancaster, Talika and Lazartigue. Based in Beijing and Los Angeles, the company has logistical activities in Beijing and Shanghai and runs major regional offices in Guangzhou, Chengdu, Chongqing, Xi'an, Dalian, Wuhan, Nanjing, Hangzhou and Qingdao. It also operates its own perfumery stores.

Shanghai Brilliance Group represents a merger of four state-owned enterprises—Shanghai Yi Bai, Hua Lian, Shanghai Friendship and Shanghai Materials—and is the largest mass-market distributor in China, with 5,000 outlets, including 2,500 super-markets, 20 department stores and six shopping malls. But it also sells luxury goods through its international distribution division, which deals with Lancel and Royal Doulton, amongst others.

Wahking Trading Co. was created in Macau in the 1990s. It distributes Trussardi products from stores in Xiamen, Taizhou and Wenzhou, and the very expensive Vertu mobile telephones from 45 points of sale in China.

Beijing-based **Catic** began as a watch distributor in 1997 and acts as the Chinese agent for brands such as Audemars Piguet, Baume et Mercier, Chopard, IWC, Jaeger-LeCoultre, Longines, Omega, Piaget, Raymond Weil, Rolex, Tag Heuer, Tissot, Vacheron

Constantin and many others. It also operates 545 watch retail stores across 25 cities.

Guangzhou Jenny Trading is a new type of distributor. It holds exclusive distribution rights (negotiated through the Hong Kong group Goldstone, which also holds a master license for Charles Jourdan, Guy Laroche and Rochas products) for Balenciaga shoes in China. The company has 150 employees. The company has a few exclusive points of sale, but most of its business is done through high-end independent points of sale (of which there were 40 in 2007).

Guangzhou Jiansheng Trading is a manufacturer of shoes and leather goods, with 120 employees in its three factories in China. It also has a license agreement with Pierre Cardin to sell Pierre Cardin shoes in approximately 1,000 points of sale. They are reported to be in the process of purchasing 100% of the worldwide Pierre Cardin group.

Run Yuan Fashion, based in Shenzhen, is again more of a licensee than a real distributor. It is the licensee for Daniel Hechter men's ready-to-wear products, but subcontracts the manufacturing in China and acts as the distribution arm in the full licensing process. It has 70 employees in Shenzhen and uses 400 sales representatives to cover the Chinese territory. It used to own three ready-to-wear factories but has separated the two activities and is now exclusively a domestic distributor. It also distributes licensed shirts and some men's leather accessories.

The six distributors mentioned above have very little in common with the Hong Kong and Singapore distributors. They import some products but are really the commercial systems linked to licensed activities.

Regional wholesalers or local distributors

Given the size of the country, another type of Chinese distributor is worth mentioning here. These are the companies that purchase products from mainland Chinese distribution subsidiaries of luxury brands and that distribute them in one part of the territory. (To cover this huge market, brands are not necessarily equipped with their own salaried sales representatives in every part of the country.)

Emilienne Cosmetics, established in Chengdu in 1999, is a "wholesaler" for foreign cosmetics brands in the south east regions of Kunming, Chengdu, Chongqing and Guiyang. It distributes L'Oréal and the affiliated Yue Sai brands in department stores and Vichy and La Roche Posay products in pharmacies. It is also acts as a wholesaler for Shisheido in the territory. A company such as this could be of interest to other brands in new luxury areas looking to distribute their products.

Guangzhou Sai Yu Trading is a distributor (or wholesaler) for the south of China. Located in Guangzhou, it has very close contacts with major luxury points of sale in Guangzhou such as the Friendship stores and La Perla. But it also covers Shanghai, Dalian, Qingdao and Kunming. It distributes Cartier and Hermes watches and Salvatore Ferragamo ready-to-wear and leather goods. It also works for Agatha. It also acts as a facilitator through its own commercial activities in southern China where, for example, it has a 10% share in the Cartier joint venture which was created to set up and manage the Cartier store in Guangzhou.

To conclude this sub-section, it has to be said that there is no single system to cover the entire Chinese territory. Different brands have different set-ups and even if they have their own subsidiary, they may use a local distributor in some parts of the country. They may also use a local "partner" to help them with their operations in a particular city or region. There are obviously many ways to operate in China, and Hong Kong and Singapore remain important points of entry.

What to look for in a Chinese distributor

There are several things to consider here:

• The size sheer size of the country dictates that there are several entry points, including Shanghai, Beijing, Hong Kong and Guangzhou.

- In the marketing plan, it may not be necessary to cover the whole country from the outset. It might make more sense to start with two stores—one in Shanghai and another in Beijing—and monitor what happens there before planning to move to other parts of the country.
- It may be necessary to use different systems in different parts of the country. A regional distributor may be a very good way to enter some areas.
- In assessing potential new distributors, it is very important to check their legal status. A fully-owned private corporation, a state-owned enterprise or a company that belongs to a private group of companies or to the local authorities presents different kinds of risk and opportunity in different parts of the country.
- It is important to understand that the brand awareness of a given brand among the Chinese population may not be the same as in other parts of the world. Brands that are very well known almost everywhere else in the world may be almost unknown in China. Or even if the brand is known, it may have a different perception or a different image among the Chinese target consumers.

ENDNOTE

1   This list is based on "le marché de luxe en Chine et à Hong Kong," UBIFRANCE, March 2007.

Shiatzy Chen

A brief history

Often referred to as China's Coco Chanel, company founder and lead designer Shiatzy Chen (Wang Chen Tsai Hsia (陈夏婆 or 王陈彩霞)) has become a veritable *tour de force* among Chinese luxury brands. Born in Taiwan in 1951, Chen served her apprenticeship as a dress-maker and then, with her husband, Wang Yuan Hong (王元宏), established a women's-wear factory, Shiatzy International Company Limited, in 1978. Following initial uncertainty ("At the beginning I wasn't sure if I had an interest in designing or not," she said in an interview. "I'm not a highly educated person, and if you don't have an education, you have to be self-reliant and have a skill. My skill was making clothes."[1]), she developed her brand in the Taiwanese market before expanding to incorporate a design studio in Paris in 1991. In 2001, she opened a boutique in Paris and then turned her attention to mainland China, where she had long harbored hopes of expanding her activities.

Development in China

Shiatzy Chen first entered the Chinese market in 2003 with the open-ing of her flagship store on the Bund in Shanghai. In addition to 39 points of sale in Taiwan in 2009, she has seven boutiques in mainland China, another in Hong Kong and, despite the current economic crisis, is well on track to achieve her aim of having 50 shops around the world by 2010. Indeed, in May 2009 she had 49 stores and employed 300 people, handling around 100,000 items of clothing a year.

Shiatzy Chen Flagship in Shanghai Bund No. 9
Copyright: Pierre Xiao Lu

Chen understands the current market situation in China, the buying patterns of the Chinese, and the potential for growth: "It's not unusual for a wealthy woman from the provinces to come to Shanghai for the day and buy every skirt in her size—spending tens of thousands of dollars in a single spree . . . more Chinese have an interest in wearing Chinese-design clothes."[2] Though most of Chen's customers are very sophisticated women, celebrities, and wives of government officials, and are generally in the over-35 age bracket, the company has begun to target a younger audience through new designs and marketing campaigns.

In 2004, the company had a turnover of roughly US$23 million[3] and we estimate its sales to be more than US$40 million in 2008. For the period 2004–08, Shiatzy Chen saw a growth of roughly 15% a year, which enabled it to quickly expand in the mainland. In addition to two Shanghai flagships, a large factory and corporate headquarters were also built, with a large portion of profits going straight into R&D and creation, and cash flow going into opening new stores.[4] In an interview before her all-important Paris fashion show, Shiatzy Chen detailed the successful transformation from a knitwear factory into a high-fashion house, "There have been a lot of things we have had to focus on in order for all this to come together. The most important thing that we've done, I feel, is to have had a very practical approach to business in terms of making sure that we are well-organized internally and that all of our employees—it doesn't matter whether they are on the design side or the corporate side—have been trained to work at an international standard. It really has involved a lot of hard work and dedication to get to this point."[5]

The product

Mixing Western craftsmanship and Eastern attention to detail—more specifically, intermixing contemporary looks with subtle influences from the Song dynasty or the five major embroidery techniques of Suzhou—Shiatzy Chen has created what has been called the "neo-Chinese chic." Her collections incorporate all four seasons, and include women's wear, men's wear, shoes and accessories, as well as home furnishings and linens. Her style has revived traditional tailoring techniques to create a modern, sleek look. Each garment has the Chinese characters"初里" (or "original intention") on each label. Her goal? "If someone looks at a piece of clothing and is able to tell at once that it is a Shiatzy Chen piece, then I know I have succeeded."[6]

The store

Although the building which houses the bigger of the Shanghai flagship stores is currently masked by the ongoing construction for the
Bund Passage, an underground traffic tunnel due for completion in
March 2010, the architect-designed interior epitomizes the contemporary retail space, fusing the contemporary with a strong sense of
Chinese tradition and culture (calligraphy adorns the walls along-
side plasma screen televisions) and in so doing captures the spirit
than runs through Shiatzy Chen's creations.

Collaboration and events

Promoting the brand through creative collaboration and events
remains vital for any fashion house. With this in mind, Shiatzy
Chen hosted a thirtieth-anniversary party in conjunction with the
Macau boutique opening with the Autumn/Winter 2008 fashion
show at the MGM Grand. For the show, which had 30 models and
an array of celebrity guests, she collaborated with Swarovski to illustrate
a design theme of "glorification." She even took advantage of the
Olympic frenzy when NBC's "Today Show" held an on-air fashion
show featuring some of her designs.

In October 2008, Shiatzy Chen made her debut at the Paris
fashion week for the new 2009 Spring/Summer collection.
There, international models showcased 50 outfits revolving around
a central design theme of Chinese porcelain.

Major issues

As the business continues to develop, with sales probably exceeding
US$40 million in 2008, Shiatzy Chen will be faced with a new set
of issues and challenges:

Shiatzy Chen Store in Beijing 2008
Copyright: Elizabeth Peng

The first issue relates to the origin of the brand. Today, apart from the one store in Paris, the brand is sold mainly in Taiwan and China, but is not clearly perceived as a Chinese or a Taiwanese brand. There is a clear need for a better definition of the brand and its creator. This could be achieved by having the name of a city attached to that of the brand. But which city? Taipei? Beijing? Shanghai? Or could it even be Paris? Should it be developed as an Asian brand, a worldwide brand or a neo-Chinese chic brand? Should the founder herself appear more in public and what story should she present to the public? Shiatzy Chen should be better known worldwide as an international brand and should command higher awareness than, for example, Shanghai Tang. But this does not seem to be the case. What could be done to improve this situation?

The second issue that needs to be addressed relates to the company's price policy. Shiatzy Chen is positioned at a very high price, almost as expensive as Chanel and probably twice as expensive as Hugo Boss. It is also significantly more expensive (up to 50% more) than Shanghai Tang, which is itself already perceived as an expensive brand. Is this the correct long-term policy to help the brand's growth in China and worldwide? Perhaps it may be necessary to come up with a lower price line to heighten customer interest? As it deals with very rich, and mainly Asian, customers, should it enlarge its price range to engage a larger group of potential consumers?

A third issue relates to its geographical development priorities. Should the brand develop in Europe? Should it develop mainly in the United States, as Shanghai Tang has done? Or should it continue to build its very strong Chinese base before going elsewhere? In that respect, the Paris store, which is probably losing money, was not necessarily such a good idea. Would a Tokyo store make more sense?

A further matter to be looked at relates to merchandising. Should it remain essentially a ready-to-wear brand or should it develop its accessories more strongly (as Shanghai Tang has done, selling small low-priced items such as notebooks or photo frames)? This is pertinent not just from the point of view of sales but also as it relates to the overall image of the brand and its specific product offerings.

ENDNOTES

1 *Taipei Times,* August 27, 2008.
2 *Taipei Times,* January 27, 2005.
3 CNN, "China's New Cultural Revolution," May 28, 2007.
4 *Taipei Times,* January 27, 2005.
5 *Taipei Times,* January 27, 2005.
6 *Taipei Times,* August 27, 2008.

CHAPTER 5

Retailing and Licensing in China

C HINA is a vast and complex country, made more complicated to the outsider by an array of municipalities, provincial cities and prefectural cities.

In its study of luxury in China,[1] KPMG presents a number of
elements that must be taken into account to measure the luxury
potential of different cities. We will first look at this, before moving
into specific descriptions of major retail scenes in China.

Where to go

In many countries, the question of where to go would not make
much sense. In China it does. As we will see in this chapter, the
Chinese market is huge, and can be approached from different
angles and different perspectives. Figure 5.1 presents a map show-
ing the locations of the major cities and while the majority of these
are on the east coast, there are many important locations in the
center and west of the country.

How many cities should you reach? For most average-size
brands, the ideal number is probably between six and eight, which
is probably the maximum a brand can afford; but it all depends on
the brand status.

As Appendix A makes clear, this is not a single market, but
a series of markets corresponding to the different tiers of cities,
which are organized in order of importance (Tier 1 for Beijing and
Shanghai, for example, and then Tiers 2a, 2b and 2c for different
cities of interest, as illustrated in Figure 5.2).

FIGURE 5.1: *Locations of major Chinese cities*

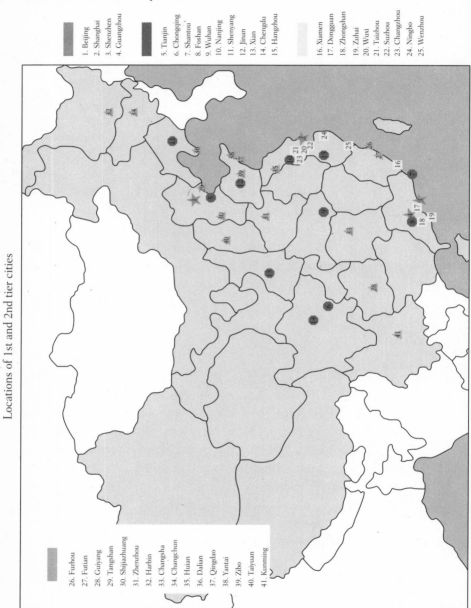

Locations of 1st and 2nd tier cities

1. Beijing
2. Shanghai
3. Shenzhen
4. Guangzhou

5. Tianjin
6. Chongqing
7. Shantou
8. Foshan
9. Wuhan
10. Nanjing
11. Shenyang
12. Jinan
13. Xian
14. Chengdu
15. Hangzhou

16. Xiamen
17. Dongguan
18. Zhongshan
19. Zuhai
20. Wuxi
21. Taizhou
22. Suzhou
23. Changzhou
24. Ningbo
25. Wenzhou

26. Fuzhou
27. Futian
28. Guiyang
29. Tangshan
30. Shijiazhuang
31. Zhenzhou
32. Harbin
33. Changsha
34. Changchun
35. Huian
36. Dalian
37. Qingdao
38. Yantai
39. Zibo
40. Taiyuan
41. Kunming

FIGURE 5.2: *Multi-tier system of Chinese cities*

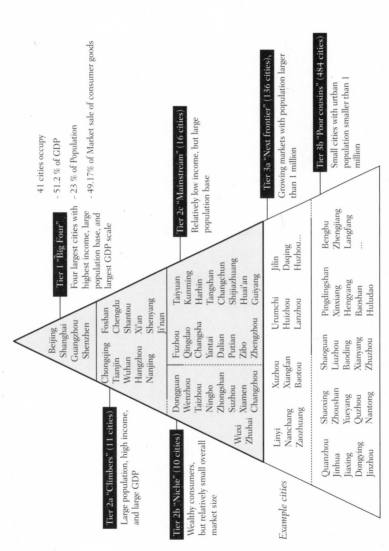

Source: *China Statistical Yearbook*; MGI analysis. Note that Tier 3b is also referred to as Tier 4. Our reference to Tier 3 combines 3a with 3b for a total of 620 cities.

The KPMG study mentioned earlier took into account the size of the adult population, the number of households with an income above US$6,500 per year, and the percentage of the population who travel overseas. It considered that with an income below US$6,500 a year, consumers cannot really indulge in buying any type of luxury goods. But it is interesting to note that above this level people can start to be in the market; which is certainly an indication of the attractiveness of luxury goods in the country.

The more Chinese citizens travel abroad, the more they are likely to encounter different brands and start to understand their underlying meaning and vision. As they come back home, they want to find the products they have seen elsewhere. With this in mind, Table 5.1 shows a breakdown of the overseas travel patterns of people in the major cities.

TABLE 5.1: *Income and overseas travel statistics for major cities (I)*

	Households (million) with annual income above US$6,500	Percentage traveling overseas	Total adult population (million)
Shenzhen	3.04	48%	5.5
Shanghai	2.98	41%	10.3
Beijing	2.78	34%	8.4
Nanjing	1.87	22%	3.1
Guangzhou	1.58	63%	6.6
Hangzhou	1.42	23%	2.1

Source: KPMG

Table 5.2 presents a similar breakdown for cities with a smaller number of households that meet the income criterion.

From Table 5.3, which shows the locations of the major luxury brands that are already in China, we can see that only Ermenegildo Zegna, Armani and Louis Vuitton have a relatively strong coverage of the country. Chanel, on the other hand, is quite late in its development and Tiffany and Prada have only a small presence. The first group of brands are not only present in stores in most of the major cities and those in the second-tier list, but are also present in third-tier cities such as Changchun, Qingdao and Kunming.

TABLE 5.2: *Income and overseas travel statistics for major cities (II)*

	Households (million) with annual income above US$6,500	Percentage traveling overseas	Total adult population (million)
Wuhan	0.90	20%	4
Chengdu	0.74	19%	3.3
Tianjin	0.63	24%	4.5
Xi'an	0.61	10%	2.6
Dalian	0.60	12%	2.7
Fuzhou	0.53	12%	1.6
Chongqing	0.54	22%	4.3
Harbin	0.40	24%	3.2
Shenyang	0.38	35%	4.1

Source: KPMG

In the first group of cities, Beijing is clearly number one, followed by Shanghai (for a more detailed analysis of these two cities, see Appendix B.) Hangzhou is a strange case because it is definitely a Tier-2a city, but some brands give it a special status. Some observers even rank it as a first-tier city. Nick Debnam and Georges Svinos from KPMG explained: "People from Hangzhou are part of the very few Chinese citizens who spend more on fashion than on food." Shenzhen, on the other hand, with more than twice the population, is comparatively weak, probably because the duty-free city of Hong Kong is very close by.

In the second tier, Chengdu, Shenyang and Tianjin figure quite prominently.

This table should prove useful as an indicator of where the opportunities currently lie.

But how expensive is it to open stores in these cities? Table 5.4 provides the answers. What can be said here is that rents for a store in a top location in Beijing are 60% cheaper than a similar rent in Tokyo.

Nevertheless, our estimate is that a store in Tokyo brings sales per square meter that are three times higher than a store in Beijing. If one considers that rents in Tokyo should reach a maximum of 20% of sales, this ratio in Beijing, considering the lower rental cost but the much lower sales per square foot, would be significantly higher.

Although rents in other Chinese cities are lower, doing business in China is not necessarily cheap and easy.

TABLE 5.3: *Location of major brands in China (by number of stores)*

	ARMANI	BULGARI	CARTIER	CHANEL	COACH	DIOR	GUCCI	HERMES	LOUIS VUITTON	PRADA	TIFFANY	ZEGNA	TOTAL
Beijing	6	3	3	2	2	3	4	3	3	3	2	4	38
Changchun	1		1			1			1			1	5
Changsha												1	1
Chengdu	1	1	1		2	1	1		1	1	1	2	12
Chongqing	1		1										2
Dalian	1					1		2	1			2	7
Fuzhou													0
Guangzhou	1	1	1			1		1	1	1		1	8
Hangzhou	1		1		1	1	1	2	1			2	10
Harbin	1		1										2
Jinan												1	1
Kunming	1		1						1			1	4
Nanjing	1	1			1	1			1			1	6
Qingdao			1		1		1		1	1			5
Sanya													1
Shangdong											1		1
Shanghai	7	1	2	1	4	2	4	1	1	1	3	4	31
Shenyang	2	1	1		1	2	1		1	1	1	2	13
Shenzhen	1		1		1		1		2			2	8
Sichuan													1
Suzhou	1						1		1			1	4
Taiyan												1	1
Tianjin	1		1			2	1	1	1		1	2	10
Wenzhou	1								1				2
Wuhan	1												1
Xi'an	1				1		1		1	1		2	7
Xiamen									1				1
Zhengzhou												1	1
Total	**31**	**8**	**16**	**3**	**14**	**14**	**17**	**10**	**21**	**9**	**9**	**31**	**183**

Source: Annual reports and company websites

TABLE 5.4: *Annual rental costs (US$) per square meter for top locations, 2007*

New York	Fifth Avenue	14,200
Hong Kong	Causeway Bay	11,500
Paris	Av. des Champs Ely.	8,700
London	New Bond Street	7,800
Tokyo	Ginza	6,500
Seoul	Gangnam Station	4,000
Beijing	Wangfujing	2,600

Source: Cushman and Wakefield, quoted in Shanghai Daily, November 20, 2007

Duty-free activities

For 2008, it is estimated that duty-free sales worldwide amounted to US$26 billion at retail value; for total luxury sales the figure was US$260 billion.[2]

In China, we estimate that all duty-free sales (at airports and seaports and for diplomats) currently account for approximately US$500 million (US$800 million if Hong Kong figures are included), and this figure is expected to grow rapidly in the next 10 years. For example, according to the World Tourism Organization, China will have 137 million foreign tourists by 2020, making it the world's leading tourist destination.[3] If each of these were to buy, say, US$20-worth of products at their departure airport (which is the current average purchase at Beijing Airport, for example), the total sales figure would clearly amount to a considerable sum.

In the same way, Chinese tourists will travel abroad in large numbers, adding to the volume of duty-free business. According to the Airports Council International, there were 4.8 billion airline passengers in 2008. China, with more than 20% of the world's population, still has considerable room to grow in this regard.

Today, most of China's international travel is concentrated at four major airports, as shown in Table 5.5.

TABLE 5.5: *Passenger traffic at major Chinese airports*

Beijing*	53,583,664 passengers (2007)
Shanghai**	51,042,419 passengers (2008)
Hong Kong*	47,042,419 passengers (2007)
Guangzhou***	30,958,467 passengers (2008)

Source: * Airports Council statistics; ** websites of Pudong and Hongqiao airports; *** airport website

Duty-free activities in China: An historical perspective

The China International Travel Service (CITS Group) was created in 1954 to develop tourism to and from China; this quickly gave rise to 14 overseas subsidiaries.

In 1984, another state company, China International Duty Free Corporation, was created, with a monopoly to purchase duty-free products abroad and to supply them to all duty-free operators in China. Initially set up as a supply and logistics company, over time it began to operate duty-free shops on its own account. It also established joint-venture arrangements with international duty-free companies whereby the international firm would bid for airport duty-free concessions and the CITS Group would handle purchasing and product supply.

In 2003, the CITS Group acquired the China International Duty Free Corporation (Renamed CDFG) to become a comprehensive operator for all domestic and overseas tourist activities.

Today, the CDFG has also developed large duty-free retail activities, operating 153 duty-free shops in 90 cities, with sales which we estimate to be in the region of US$200 million. By 2004, the CDFG was the sole purchasing agent and had supply arrangements and partnership contracts with almost everybody in the industry. This has changed somewhat today, as each operator is able to run the show in its own way. In fact, the CDFG generally operates in smaller airports (which are often unprofitable), while the larger international groups concentrate on major sites. But even though the foreign operators can now purchase their products directly, they have to maintain a good relationship with CDFG, which retains overall control. For example, when at the end of 2007 the CDFG introduced a strong price-reduction campaign (of up to 20%) to increase duty-free sales volumes, all other operators were obliged to follow suit.

The major operators

The strongest operator is Sunrise, a Taiwanese retailer, which operates the two major airports of Beijing and Pudong. We estimate its sales turnover in China to be around US$200 million.

In 2005, Sunrise won the tender to operate 2,300 square meters of retail space in Beijing (the airport authorities keeping 700 square meters to themselves). Against strong competition from the CDFG, Orient King Power, Shenzhen Duty Free and the Nuance Group, it won a 10-year concession, committing to a minimum annual concession fee of US$23.4 million. Sunrise expected to reach sales of US$50 million fairly rapidly and by 2008 its recorded sales were US$34 million.[4]

Sunrise began its operations at Shanghai's Pudong airport in 1999, when it was awarded a 10-year concession for duty-free tobacco sales. In 2001, it expanded its business to include fragrances and cosmetics and now deals with wines and spirits, and fashion accessories as well.

In Hong Kong, the airport duty-free concession is operated by the Nuance Watson Partnership, a joint venture between the Zurich-based Nuance Group—the second-most powerful duty-free operator worldwide, with sales of US$1.7 billion—and the Watson retailing group based in Hong Kong. In addition to the usual duty-free activities, the Partnership also has special boutiques for Bally, Bulgari, Hugo Boss, Longchamp and Omega, and is in the process of building the first Armani duty-free store. In 2007, it recorded sales of US$320 million. It also operates out of Macau and Zhuhai airports.

The Guangzhou airport concession was awarded to the CDFG in 2008, with a 10-year contract to manage 1,000 square meters of retail space and operate nine stores. Its major activities are in watches, fragrances and cosmetics, and fashion boutiques such as Salvatore Ferragamo, Bally, dunhill, Shanghai Tang, Tumi and Furla.

As for other duty-free locations, Duty Free Shoppers (DFS) runs Hainan Meilan Airport on a 10-year concession awarded in 2005 (which also includes a duty-paid retail activity); and King Power Duty Free operates some Shanghai outlets.

The downtown stores

The CDF Group operates downtown duty-free stores located in major cities, where tourists can browse and select products and then pick them up at the airport on their way home. These stores were opened when the CDF Group still had the monopoly on the sourcing of foreign duty-free products. The first was opened in Beijing in 1990, and was followed by others in Shanghai (1999), Dalian (2003), and Qingdao and Xiamen (2005). We estimate that 70% of downtown duty-free consumers are Japanese.

Licensing[5]

Introduction

China will probably not follow the same development path as Japan, which paid a high price to obtain licensee contracts in the 1970s and '80s. The Japanese understood that their fashions and styles were very specific to their own culture and that it would take them a lot longer to influence the fashion world than it had taken them to exert an influence on electronic products or cameras, for instance.

The Japanese learned very quickly that while their domestic market was interested in buying Western styles, it would be diffi-cult to find good local designers capable of producing those styles. Licensing, therefore, was clearly the best way to learn from Western brands, and to adapt those styles to the Japanese taste.

Having said that, China is much less likely to develop a Chinese style because many local brands are developing their styles in a more global Western way. While this may make it easier for Western brands to be accepted, it also exposes them to greater competition from local brands, the more ambitious of which may use the very powerful production capabilities available to them to export their styles and brands around the world.

The Chinese and Western perceptions of licensing are quite different. It can work but both parties may have different objectives.

Western perceptions of licensing in China

While it is fair to say that licensing in China does not have a good reputation, the actual number of licensee contracts is not huge and most people in the branding business do not have a bad story to tell. Licensing entails providing a brand and a design to a specific company on an exclusive basis for that company to manufacture and distribute the licensed products in a specified territory. The major concern for most Western brands is that unscrupulous local licensees may use the license to export the licensed products beyond the remit of the original contract. However, such activities will quickly become obvious to the brand and, if they continue, lead to the licensee losing the business and/or having legal proceedings taken against it. But such occurrences are rare and easily curtailed when they come to light.

The second issue which concerns the Western/international brand is the design of the licensee products. We highly recommend that 100% design should come from the licensor. In fashion products, however, a licensee would normally use 70% of the licensed collection and then propose some additional styles or changes to the remainder. Such changes and additions require the complete approval of the licensor.

The third issue is manufacturing. Many international brands do manufacture in China because they know that it is entirely possible to manufacture high quality products here. While a licensee may prefer to use its own factory or its usual subcontractors, it is preferable if the licensee uses the same factories used by the licensor for its worldwide production. This ensures that quality standards are maintained, that the right materials will be available without having to worry about minimum-quantity concerns, and that the licensee will have to spend less time on instructing and supervising the manufacturer.

Samples of the local production will need to be sent to the licensor for approval but the quantities will vary, depending on the relationship between the licensor, its local representative (which we recommend having) and the licensee.

We believe that the main issue in licensing is one of price and overall brand positioning. Licensing, even if it means paying royalties (6–12% of the wholesale value), enables goods to be produced at a lower cost than if they were imported. The licensee (who is also the distributor) may be tempted to lower the retail price in order to reach breakeven faster. However, this may have the effect of positioning the brand too low. Once this happens, it will become almost impossible to rectify the positioning in the future. Naturally, it can be pointed out to the licensee that it is in its own interests to keep a high selling price to make more margin once the business is running well; but it is not always possible for the licensor to impose its own view.

By the same logic, licensees who rely on a cheaper price to sell are also likely to spend less in media/communication/PR than should be done. We recommend defining a specific amount per season to be spent and checking all expenses.

It is difficult to make new licensing agreements in China where the licensee has sole responsibility for making investments in products, points of sale, advertising, and so on. One way around this would be to reduce the level of royalties required of the licensee, or to share part of the investment costs. For example, the licensor may agree to pay half the rent of a flagship store (if the store loses money, the losses would be shared by both parties). Where the licensor makes some investment of this kind, it will have a much greater chance of ensuring that the brand is correctly positioned.

With this in mind, it might be interesting for a Western brand to open its own shop in China, to learn how to adapt merchandising to the local market, and then be in a stronger position to negotiate with local companies in selecting a local licensee and distributor.

In addition to ensuring minimum royalties per season, this would also make it possible to determine accurate turnover figures, which then could allow checking whether the licensee should pay additional royalties.

In China, most of a brand's distribution would be in department stores. The brand should ensure that under the terms of its licensing contracts with the stores, it has access to detailed and accurate information on each store's monthly turnover and margins. Having such precise information makes it easier to then estimate turnover in other points of sale.

Chinese perceptions of licensing

Naturally in a country of the size and diversity of China, there are all kinds of mentalities and many local groups are not interested in licensing, preferring instead to focus on building their own brands in their own market, which could then be exported to foreign countries.

However, such groups have mistakenly believed that middle-class consumption in China would blossom much faster than has actually been the case. There is indeed a middle-class but its purchasing power has been far outstripped by that of the rich. As a result, department-stores and shopping malls have given up waiting for the middle-class boom to eventuate and have upgraded their floors in order to attract more high-end brands catering to the rich. In the process, many local brands have been pushed away and their only real access to the higher-end department stores is through becoming a licensee for foreign brands. Their motives and aims for doing so are thus often quite different from those of the Western brands with which they enter into licensing agreements and can lead to misunderstanding in the mid-to-long term.

It is essential, therefore, when discussing or negotiating with local groups that the international brand understands their real purpose in taking a license and whether this has the potential to conflict with its own brand goals.

Having already learned from experience, many potential Chinese licensees are wary of becoming involved with Western brands, fearing that the brands are only interested in licensing as a way of learning about distribution and that once this has been mastered the licensing agreement will not be renewed. This has happened and will happen again in China, much more than in other Asian countries, because of the strategic aspect of the market.

This can be partly resolved through negotiation. Perhaps, for example, the licensor could guarantee automatic renewal of the contract if all royalty arrangements have been met in full.

Another way for the licensor to motivate the licensee is to offer to buy products from him. Export activities have been China's main business for the last 40 years but export margins have shrunk. It is good, therefore, for a licensee to produce both for its own market, as a licensee, and for export to the licensor. This will encourage greater product cooperation and improve the quality of the product to be sold locally. However, the licensor should not be obliged to buy from the licensee; otherwise, prices would not be reasonable.

In the future, we may see new types of cooperation between licensee and licensor, where the licensor would become the importer-distributor of the licensee's own local brand. Discussions along these lines are already taking place and it may not be long before they come to fruition in Europe, the United States and Japan.

Licensing is a very good and effective means for a licensee to learn all aspects of the brand, including manufacturing. It may well be that we will soon see Chinese licensees confident enough to buy the licensor's whole operation.

Evolution and profile of licensee companies

In the early 1990s, it was not practical to use local Chinese companies as licensee partners since they were not able to comply with legal/financial issues and lacked an understanding of both licensing and the marketing concept. Hong Kong and Taiwanese companies, on the other hand, had had many years' experience in their own markets and enjoyed a better reputation in compliance terms.

China's economy has developed mostly through its export business and will continue to do so; in 2008, domestic activities contributed just 35% of its GDP growth. In the '80s, the majority of business came from state-owned enterprises (SOEs). Being both state-owned and mostly industrial, they had little knowledge of domestic marketing, especially since they enjoyed a monopoly in a few provinces. Impressed by the size and power of such local groups, some international brands dealt with SOEs but real cooperation proved to be difficult because it wasn't possible to build proper marketing teams and the SOEs were reluctant to spend on promotion or to give the proper authority to brand managers.

Today, SOEs contribute one-quarter of China's economy. While those which survived have made a great deal of progress and could be suitable for licensing agreements—particularly in manufacturing—their weak points in marketing, merchandising and promotion remain.

Private export-oriented companies often have similar problems since they too have kept a manufacturing culture more than a marketing one. Many of them have been tremendously successful in the export business, and have then turned to producing for the local market as well, and to becoming distributors rather than wholesalers. In short, their management would always think that buying a new machine is a better investment than renting a flagship store in Shanghai. They often have difficulties developing brand value. This isn't helped by the fact that many keep their head office at the factory site, making it impossible to attract marketing, designer or merchandising teams who have no interest in living in a dormitory or in having to commute a few hours a day.

Local companies which have developed successful brands on their own and may be interested in launching a foreign brand often experience difficulties in choosing the best complementary brand to add to their existing portfolio. They may also have conflicting objectives: whether to promote their own brands first or to invest more in a foreign brand which has good potential in the China market.

Then there are the truly marketing-oriented companies. These may well have started out in the export business but have moved away from the ownership of factories, preferring subcontracting, allocating more resources in marketing, opening boutiques or corners, and spending on communication, advertising and PR. While such companies present better options than those outlined above, they are less likely to persist if the brand proves more difficult to promote than expected.

Hong Kong and Taiwanese companies have now had more than 20 years of experience of operating under license in China and have a track record that can be checked. For many years, Hong Kong licensees have managed the China market from Hong Kong, without having a sufficient understanding of the local issues and the diversity of different provinces. They have tended to believe that their experience in Hong Kong is equally applicable in main-land China. They were good in promotion but less so in merchan-dising and HR management. Coming from a strong stock-market culture, many have provided exciting business plans and, expecting to be listed on the Hong Kong stock market, have tried to fast-track development in the China market. Their growth has been too fast, as attested to by the many bankruptcies recorded in the last two or three years.

The ones which have succeeded are those which moved their operations to China (mostly Shanghai), combining their market-ing knowledge and experience from Hong Kong with a deeper local understanding.

Not surprisingly given their history, the Taiwanese have been much faster in gaining an understanding of local culture, management and diversity. Taiwan has a strong industrial culture and began setting up high-quality factories in China in the early 1990s. Though not as advanced as Hong Kong in branding, neither were they intent on getting listed on the stock market. Those companies are generally still operating and are very safe.

For licensors reviewing potential licensing partners, it is important to be aware of their background, which will reveal more about their true strengths and weaknesses. While all of the options outlined above may make for suitable partnerships, only the individual licensors can decide on what is the best fit for their particular long-term operations and plans.

How to choose a licensee

Given the size of China, most companies are strongest in their specific province of origin. While it would seem logical to have two or three different licensees to cover the entire country, thus far licensees have been reluctant to become involved in such an arrangement, feeling that the initial investment costs of merchandising and building brand awareness is too great.

Usually, licensees (as well as importer-distributors) have their offices in Shanghai, Beijing, and Guangzhou, where they open corners in department stores or boutiques in shopping malls. This is essential to build a coherent image in the most prestigious cities and to gather practical, everyday experience of how to improve turnover.

It is also essential to build a model to motivate provincial distributors and franchisees. On average, licensees have direct control of over 30% of their points of sale. The remaining 70% would be subject to direct franchising or distribution contracts in each province. These distributors would, like the licensees themselves, have direct control of a few points of sale in the biggest cities in the province, and franchisees in other places.

Because franchising is very common in China, licensees know that they will be able to rely on them (directly or through distributors) and ask licensors to give them an exclusive license in China since they have a way to cover all territories.

The following are the key points to consider in selecting a licensee partner:

- In branding, price positioning is essential. In licensing, having too low a price is the highest of all risks. If the licensor's brand positioning in China is more than 30% higher than the other brands distributed by the licensee, it will be difficult for the licensee to build a marketing team to match those expectations and to reach the new consumers necessary to maintain that higher position.

- If the licensor requires the brand to have a strong presence in department stores, it would help to have a licensee who already has experience of distributing in department stores. Building relationships with department stores from scratch would need a lot of time and resources.

- Having a licensee whose top marketing management is sensitive to the product and to its specific promotional and personnel needs is very important. In the Chinese culture, a contract is not a document to follow on a daily basis. On a daily basis, the trust between the licensor, the licensor's local representative, and the licensee are essential, together with a continuous reminder of what has been agreed in the business plan. If this does not work, the terms of the contract will need to be reviewed and amended, as necessary.

- The licensee merchandiser (who decides which of the licensor's products will be sold locally) and the designer (who will propose some additional styles to be approved by the licensor) are both important people. The licensee needs to demonstrate an ability to hire people of the required quality.

- Store management is very important. The sales staff hired by the licensee will likely focus on selling, without paying much attention to the way the products are displayed. The licensor therefore needs to have arrangements in place to visit each point of sale on a weekly basis to ensure that the products are being promoted in a manner that is coherent with the brand image.

- In a national distribution network, the licensee will generally rely on provincial distributors and franchisees. However, franchisees cannot be trusted with merchandising. The licensor must insist that the licensee's agreement with franchisees covers only obtaining the right points of sale, not managing them. The licensor must insist that all merchandising activities and all training of franchisees' sales staff should be done by the licensee.

Brands with multiple product categories

Licensing can offer the possibility of increasing the number of the Western brand's product categories, where this may not be possible in the original market. Japan offers a clear example of this. Many Western brands had master contracts with large Japanese conglomerates, which would partially develop some categories on their own and partially sub-contract other categories to long-term partners or subsidiaries. While the thought of having to deal with just one group may be convenient and appealing to Western brands, a proliferation of sub-companies under a master contract can make matters more complex than at first appears.

Few, if any, Chinese companies compare in size or power with these huge Japanese groups—not even the SOEs which, in any event, are rendered ineligible for any real consideration for a master license contract because of their limited approach to marketing. For these reasons, we have not seen much movement in the direction of developing master licensees. It seems safer (and more profitable in royalties) to have separate contracts with a specialized licensee in each product category (ready-to-wear, leather goods, fashion accessories, and so on). However, not having a master licensee makes setting up a flagship store, where all the product categories can be sold together, much more problematic. It may be possible, however, for a licensor to motivate the ready-to-wear licensee to open such a flagship or to co-invest in such a boutique with a few licensees. To promote the brand, in addition to each licensee promoting their specific products, the licensor could use part of its royalties to make such an investment.

Once a brand becomes known in one category in China, it is easier than in Western countries to use the brand name to develop additional categories. However, as we said earlier, the design should still largely come from the licensor.

Conclusion

Licensing can be as valuable to a brand as direct export activities in a new market, but this requires the licensor to have knowledgeable and dedicated staff who are capable of organizing all aspects of the brand and ensuring that these are fully explained to the licensee.

Good licensees will ask for maximum information and support from the licensor and will openly discuss how to adapt such support to their local market. Daily communication between the licensor, the licensor's representative and the licensee is vital to ensure that the original brand concept is maintained.

ENDNOTES

1   KPMG, "China's luxury consumers: Moving up the curve," 2007.
2   See Chevalier and Mazzalovo 2008.
3   "Duty-free Shop Opens at Shanghai Stadium," eastday.com, November 19, 2001; accessed via www.china.org.cn.
4   *Trend*, Travel Retail Executive News Digest, January 2009.
5   This section was written with the assistance of Christophe Laurent, General Manager of Asia Elan Corp.

Louis Vuitton in China

A brief history

Louis Vuitton, or "LV" as it is known to the Chinese, is a major division of the French holding company LVMH. Internationally recognized for its exclusivity, fine craftsmanship, and high prices, its success in the industry has been unparalleled, with its leather accessories and trunks reaching iconic status. Louis Vuitton has subsequently become one of the most counterfeited contemporary luxury brands.

The company takes its name from its founder, a nineteenth-century Frenchman who became an apprentice *layettier* (one whose occupation was to pack trunks) to prominent households, including that of Napoleon III of France who appointed Vuitton as *layettier* to his wife, Empress Eugenie. Vuitton began his own company in 1854, making large leather trunks and luggage. Such was his success that he opened his first store in London in 1855. In 1888, he produced his first classic signature pattern *damier*, a checkerboard print of light and dark contrasting brown squares. From the *damier*, came his most identifiable and popular selling canvas, the Monogram, in 1896.

LVMH in China

The LVMH group entered the Chinese market in 1992 with the unveiling of its first Louis Vuitton boutique in Beijing's Palace Hotel at a time when the Chinese market still had strict regulations concerning foreign companies and their product distribution. (China had yet to join the World Trade Organization and rules hindering the development of foreign companies were to stay in force until 2004. Only then did it become possible to build mixed-capital companies with major foreign participation in the retail sector.)

Since most multinational companies knew the potential of the Chinese market and assumed that China would enter the WTO in the near future, they began to adopt different market-entrance strategies.

The market

The Chinese luxury consumer market remains the most dynamic and promising market for fashion and luxury goods in the world. Despite the effects of the recent global economic downturn, affluent consumers continue to emerge, flexing their purchasing power in the luxury goods market. China currently accounts for 5% of global luxury sales and is growing exponentially.

For the Louis Vuitton brand, Japanese customers probably represent 50% of total sales, and other Asian customers probably account for an additional 10–15%. While the Japanese market has already matured but still manages to set the tone and surpass previous records, markets such as South Korea, Indonesia, Malaysia, and Singapore have emerged, and China in particular is well on its way to becoming the biggest market in the world.

Chinese consumers

Chinese consumers are quickly discovering luxury brands and LVMH has been quick to respond to their needs. In 1997, five years after entering the Chinese market, it opened its official Chinese website, which now also operates in English, French and Japanese.

Because of the increasing quantity and range of its seasonal products, the shelf-life of products in each season has been shortened. Luxury brands in China launch fashionable goods more frequently and in greater quantities. Louis Vuitton offers smaller products (small leather goods such as wallets or pouches, for example) in China, which have lower retailing prices. More affordable luxury or value-oriented luxury models target younger and new clientele.

Building a strong brand

Various surveys have shown that Louis Vuitton commands strong brand awareness in China. For example, in 2006, Shanghai's *Daily Economic News* conducted a survey of luxury consumption habits in Shanghai. The survey, covering 40,000 high-end consumers, found that when asked to cite a luxury brand, 72% of consumers immediately responded with "Louis Vuitton." Other questions and responses included the following:

TABLE 1: *How did you familiarize yourself with luxury goods?*

Magazines	51%
Internet	32%
Friends	10%
TV	7%

TABLE 2: *Where do you buy luxury products?*

Local high-end shopping malls	35%
Luxury brand boutiques	36%
Overseas shopping	27%
Others	2%

TABLE 3: *What price range is affordable for one piece of luxury item?*

More than US$800	6%
US$500–800	11%
US$250–500	45%
US$125–250	38%

TABLE 4: *The spontaneous recall of luxury brands*

Louis Vuitton	72%
Christian Dior	48%
Gucci	46%
Hugo Boss	21%
Chanel	19%

An ACNielsen survey in 2007 found that Louis Vuitton was one of the five most popular luxury brands in the Asia Pacific, along with Ralph Lauren, Giorgio Armani, Christian Dior, and DKNY. It was the second-most popular brand in China (with a vote of 13%), behind Chanel (15%) and ahead of Versace (12%). In Hong Kong, though, it commanded 23% of the vote.

The survey also found that when consumers in the Asia-Pacific were asked to name their favorite brands without having to give any consideration to price or affordability, Louis Vuitton was equal first with Gucci (with 32%) and ahead of Giorgio Armani (28%).

That the group commands such high brand awareness among consumers in China, and especially in Hong Kong, is in large part due to its marketing strategy, which focuses on the following four aspects:

Creating the brand's DNA

Brand building in the luxury business remains a far more complex task than meets the eye. The formula devised by Bernard Arnault, LVMH's CEO and Executive Director, goes something like this: sharply define the brand identity—or "DNA," as he puts it—by mining the brand's history and finding the right designer to express it; tightly control the quality and distribution; and finally, create a masterful marketing buzz. Arnault's formula worked so successfully that, thanks to Louis Vuitton, LVMH is able to post a large and growing operating profit every year.

Louis Vuitton's brand image is deeply rooted in a tradition that respects high quality and superb craftsmanship. The company probably employs between 8,000 and 10,000 people, each of whom is required to understand the company's history and culture, which carries with it the brand's spirit: the art of travel. All sales staff are sent to Paris to receive appropriate training. The decor of its stores and the attention paid to customer service also reflect the company's traditions.

The company has consistently pursued a luxury pricing strategy of high markups, limited availability and few, if any, markdowns, so as not to devalue the brand in the eyes of customers.

Public relations activities

Louis Vuitton organizes a multitude of public relations events to promote its brand throughout China. For example, in September 2004, to celebrate its 150th anniversary, the company opened a flagship store in Shanghai's Plaza 66, complete with a massive fête. At the party, at which more than 9,000 products were on display, the champagne flowed for the 1,500 invited guests.

As part of an art exhibition held in honor of the Sino-French cultural year 2004/05, Louis Vuitton organized a special tour of the exhibition, displaying some of its own rare collectibles. In addition, the company hosted a more intimate invitation-only party of 100 VIP guests, bringing a sense of exclusivity to these privileged few. Similar PR events have been held in Shanghai and Beijing every year since then.

For its fashion shows in Asia, Louis Vuitton selects and recruits Chinese celebrities to be ambassadors for the brand (for example, Faye Wong, Karen Mok and Du Juan).

Advertising

Since maintaining an upscale image is vital for a luxury brand, Louis Vuitton devotes more than 10% of its annual sales purely for promotional and advertising purposes. The company advertises its brands primarily in high-fashion and lifestyle magazines. Most of the leading brands are associated in one way or another with major international events with luxury cachet, and Louis Vuitton is no exception, sponsoring the America's Cup. In all of these activities, it is very careful to ensure that the image it portrays is entirely consistent with the brand image.

In March 2008, the company launched a 90-second advertisement on five television channels belonging to the Shanghai Media Group. It is interesting to note that there was no mention of the product in the ad, which simply introduced the concept of the art of travel and the impact of how travel changes lives. This was the first time Louis Vuitton ads had appeared on China's television screens and led very quickly to others appearing on a host of other channels in the more developed cities in China and in Hong Kong.

Customer response marketing (CRM) transnational management

With a comprehensive database of consumer information, Louis Vuitton closely observes the Chinese consumer. Whenever a Chinese customer buys a product in one of its overseas stores, Louis Vuitton China is notified immediately. In this way, the system enables the company to get a better understanding of the needs of its customers and to respond accordingly.

Building a retailing network

Though Louis Vuitton opened its first store in Hong Kong in 1982, it took a further 10 years before it opened its first store in Beijing. It

TABLE 5: *Louis Vuitton stores in China*

Beijing	Louis Vuitton Beijing Seasons Louis Vuitton The Peninsula Beijing Louis Vuitton Beijing China World*
Shanghai	Louis Vuitton Shanghai Plaza 66*
Chengdu	Louis Vuitton Chengdu Seibu
Dalian	Louis Vuitton Shangri-La Dalian Hotel
Guangzhou	Louis Vuitton Guangzhou La Perle
Hangzhou	Louis Vuitton Hangzhou
Kunming	Louis Vuitton Kunming Gingko Center
Nanjing	Louis Vuitton Nanjing Deji Plaza
Qingdao	Louis Vuitton Qingdao
Shenyang	Louis Vuitton Shenyang Charter Louis Vuitton Shenyang Seibu
Shenzhen	Louis Vuitton Shenzhen Seibu Louis Vuitton Shenzhen Seibu Citic
Tianjin	Louis Vuitton Tianjin You Yi
Wenzhou	Louis Vuitton Wenzhou Noble
Xi'an	Louis Vuitton Xi'an Zhong Da
Sanya	Louis Vuitton Sanya Yalong Bay
Changchun	Louis Vuitton Changchun Charter Centre
Xiamen	Louis Vuitton Xiamen Marco Polo

A flagship store.

had 21 stores in early 2008 (see Table 5) in mainland China (with another seven currently under construction and to be opened before the end of 2009), and six stores in Taiwan and Hong Kong.

All of the stores are strategically placed in the city center or in main commercial districts and, while the inventory in each may vary according to local demand, each usually operates 12 hours a day, closing only on the first day of Chinese New Year.

Buying Louis Vuitton abroad

At the opening of Louis Vuitton's landmark Hong Kong store in 2005, the CEO, Yves Carcelle, said that China (including Hong Kong) had become the company's third-largest market, with approximately 7.5% of its worldwide sales. However, he failed to include sales from Chinese traveling abroad. Now, in 2009, stores in greater China contribute around 15%, to which should be added the Chinese purchases made in other parts of the world.

A large number of Chinese tourists prefer to buy their Louis Vuitton products in Europe, where the prices are lower than those found in China. In addition, Chinese tourists have a huge inclination towards gift-giving, something almost fundamental in traditional culture. The general thought process when a Chinese tourist visits France almost automatically includes a visit to Louis Vuitton and (where possible) a memorable purchase. Though no real figures have been released regarding the percentage of the company's sales made to Chinese or Asian tourists, it is almost vital for Louis Vuitton to establish points of sale in mainland China to nurture its lifelong consumers (and not simply those who buy once in a while when on vacation).

The retailing network in China

Regardless of the ever-increasing demand for its products, Louis Vuitton opens new stores prudently and in accordance with its own calculated schedule. It exercises strict control over the number of stores it operates across the world, its main concern being to ensure that each store is able to meet and maintain the LV global standard.

Initially in China, the company opened stores in five-star hotels— the only places to find luxury goods: the Peninsula in Beijing, the Hilton in Chengdu, the Marriott China Hotel in Guangzhou, the Shangri-La in Dalian and the Portman Ritz-Carlton in Shanghai. It has since expanded into high-end shopping malls such as Shanghai's Plaza 66 and into second-tier cities such as Shenzhen, Zhuhai, Wenzhou and Hangzhou, where consumers are developing strong brand awareness and levels of disposable income that enable them to pursue their luxury interests.

Product portfolio

LV's product portfolio covers both men and women and includes luggage and other leather goods, ready-to-wear clothing and accessories, shoes, watches and jewelry, sunglasses, and writing materials. Its range of handbags and briefcases are the most popular. But with all of its products, Louis Vuitton offers a range of services including special orders, customization, and product care and repairs.

Louis Vuitton Store in Hangzhou, Zhejiang Province, China
Copyright: Pierre Xiao Lu

Major issues

In looking at the performance of Louis Vuitton in China, it is necessary to analyze the brand's situation in relation to other, comparable, brands as revealed in the various studies and surveys mentioned above. For example, when asked to name their favorite brand, Chinese respondents gave Chanel as number 1, ahead of Louis Vuitton and Versace. Yet, when asked the same question but "without consideration for money," Louis Vuitton came out on top, registering more than twice as many favorable responses as in the earlier question.

These answers are all the more puzzling when we compare the spontaneous recall of luxury brands, where Louis Vuitton came out well ahead of Christian Dior (48%) and Chanel (19%). Yet from a spontaneous awareness level of 72%, Louis Vuitton was mentioned as the "most popular brand" by only 13% of respondents, while for Chanel, which has yet to establish a major presence in China and remains extremely "aspirational," this figure was 15%. It would seem that while it is easily available and most probably the strongest brand, Louis Vuitton may not be the brand Chinese consumers still dream of.

The fact that the brand performs twice as well when money is not mentioned raises another question: Are Louis Vuitton products perceived as being extremely expensive (which they are not) or too cheap to be the real epitome of a top luxury brand. This is a question that must be addressed and, if necessary, corrective measures should be taken.

Traditionally, luxury brands have concentrated their efforts in advertising to limited-circulation, glossy fashion magazines to reach part of their upscale target consumers. But in a country like China, where distribution, even for Louis Vuitton, remains scattered, perhaps the major thrust of any communication program should be concentrated around public relations activities close to individual store locations.

When a brand has a 72% spontaneous-awareness rating, the main communication objectives probably should be to improve or modify the content of this awareness and to determine how exactly the Louis Vuitton brand is perceived by Chinese consumers. On further consideration, it may be that TV advertising is more appropriate than print advertisements, depending on specific circumstances. Another, related, question the company may need to address is whether its advertising in China should concentrate exclusively on the "art of travel" or whether it should be more product-oriented.

A third issue has to deal with the CRM system. As mentioned above, Louis Vuitton China can trace the purchases of its products by Chinese consumers in China and elsewhere. This provides management with very interesting statistics on the real volume of sales to Chinese consumers, in China and abroad, and enables an assessment to be made of the level of sales made elsewhere in the world but attributable to the specific marketing and promotional efforts made in China.

But the main question in this regard relates to how best to gear its promotional programs towards different categories of consumers. There should, perhaps, be three different programs: one for those who always buy their products in the same store (and the promotional program should be linked to that store); another for those who live in China but buy most of their Louis Vuitton goods abroad (the program should deal with them and communicate to them in China, although they are apparently not heavy buyers there); and a third should specifically address those who buy in different stores. The question in this last category is whether to put these clients on a promotional program linked to one store, or to have a mixed promotional system which issues them with invitations from different stores.

A last issue relates to the ideal long-term geographical set-up of Louis Vuitton in China. Should the main objective be to increase the "reach" and to be present in as many locations as possible? How far can availability be a very positive brand value? Or perhaps the main objective should be to concentrate on the major markets and establish itself as the biggest and highest luxury brand in China. In other words, should the company open new stores in Chongqing or Harbin, or should it open further stores in Beijing or Shanghai? Future sales volume will no doubt provide the answer to this question but it can also have different consequences for the standing of the Louis Vuitton brand and for its identity for Chinese consumers.

CHAPTER 6

Communication and Advertising

C OMMUNICATION AND ADVERTISING are always the key issues for branding in any market. But for a fashion and luxury company, communication is extremely important for success in a market such as China. The communication models are the same as anywhere else in the world, but the challenge is how to apply these effectively in China. Standardized policies may be effective in some cases but in China localization is the key, although it is not automatically suitable for every case.

In order to better explain the differences in communication and advertising for a fashion or luxury brand in China, we start with an overview of the possible communication tools available to luxury brands. We then discuss the communication models in marketing and their applications in the luxury industry in China, before focusing on some effective brand strategies that have been used at different stages of development in the market.

Communication overview

As in Europe or the U.S., the communication tools available to luxury brands in China are magazines, newspapers and outdoor media. But the difference with China lies in the number of publications, their coverage and people's interests. For example, magazines such as *People* and *Paris Match* are, at best, extremely hard to come by. In fact, all stories about movie stars or celebrities are reported in general newspapers.

It shouldn't be forgotten that China is still a Communist country and exercises strict control over media content and images. This is unlikely to be liberalized in the near future. Indeed, one commentator has suggested that international companies should resign themselves to a future of heavy regulation, strict censorship, and monopolistic or oligopolistic prices.[1] The kind of exposure of the private lives of celebrities, politicians or entrepreneurs that occurs in the media in Hong Kong or Taiwan, for example, is not allowed in China. However, despite the restrictions, it is not impossible for a luxury brand to communicate its message effectively and successfully, as the experience of many companies has shown. It is essential, though, to have a thorough understanding of the workings of the local media.

The press

Developments in information technology have meant that major foreign magazines have been able to establish a firm foothold in the Chinese domestic market, particularly among the elite, who have easy access to magazines such as *WE*, *Elle*, *Vogue* and *Cosmopolitan*, and to influential business publications such as the *Financial Times*, the *Wall Street Journal*, *Newsweek*, *Time* and *BusinessWeek*.

While no foreign publishers are allowed to publish in China, many actively participate in China's booming magazine market in the form of "cooperation," though the law prohibits them from running the editorial side of such publications. Through establishing partnerships with local businesses, many already have Chinese versions of their magazines published in the mainland market. The most influential of these include *Vogue China*, *Elle China*, *Cosmopolitan China*, *Bazaar China* and *Marie Claire China*. Major local fashion magazines include *Ruili* and *Xinwei*.

In the business and finance field, *Fortune China*, *Forbes China*, and *Harvard Business Review China* also play an important role in contributing to the international quality of articles and analysis.

High-quality Chinese business magazines and newspapers such as *China Entrepreneur*, *21st Century Business Herald*, and *Economic Observer* also attract very high numbers of subscribers.

Other influential lifestyle publications available include *Tatler*, *Noblesse*, *Modern Weekly*, and *Vision*.

The majority of these publications have international renown and need no further explanation here. It is worth mentioning, though, that since entering China in 1987 (the first international fashion magazine to do so) **Elle China** has become widely recognized as the most authoritative magazine featuring fashion, beauty and lifestyle. It is also the best media partner for premium brands to reach young, well-educated and affluent female consumers.

Of the local fashion magazines, **Ray Li** has the strongest marketing system, with showcase terminals nationwide, giving it the most effective regional coverage over markets in region-level cities and above, as well as in counties with advanced developments.

The most influential fashion and lifestyle magazines for men include *FHM*, *Vogue*, *Bazaar Men*, *Trends Esquire*, *L'officiel Hommes* and *Men's Uno China*.

Details of China's magazine market can be found in Appendix C.

Television

Many of the leading international luxury brands—Cartier, Hennessy, Remy Martin, Chivas, Johnnie Walker, Rolex, Chanel Perfumes and Dior j'adore—used television to advertise themselves when they entered the Chinese market. It is noticeable that these are mainly cosmetics or spirits brands, rather than fashion brands. In fact, very few fashion brands have chosen to communicate via television. This is not because the medium is unsuitable for building brand awareness for the fashion industry; quite the contrary, in fact. The problem is that the huge expense involved makes it uneconomic for fashion brands which, in any event, can benefit from the free TV news coverage of fashion shows and other promotional events.

The CCTV Group

China Central Television, commonly known as CCTV (simplified Chinese: 中国中央电视台 ; pinyin: Zhōngguó Zhōngyāng Diànshìtái), is the major television broadcaster in mainland China. It is a statutory agency within the State Administration of Radio, Film, and Television, which is subordinate to the State Council. Its editorial independence is subject to government policy considerations.

CCTV came on air in 1958. By the end of the 1970s, it still had only one channel, with only evening broadcasting, which usually ended at midnight.

Today, CCTV has a network of 18 channels and reaches more than a billion viewers on the Chinese mainland. Most have 24-hour broadcasting and many show popular U.S. programs such as "CSI: New York," "CSI: Miami," "24" and "Lost," as well as documentaries, movies, and new Chinese television series shot in HD.

Whilst its news reporting is regulated, most of its programming is a mix of documentaries, comedy, entertainment and drama (largely Chinese soap operas). When CCTV had its state subsidy reduced dramatically in the 1990s, it was obliged to sell commercial advertising.

CCTV has found itself competing with local television stations (also state-run) which have been creating increasingly large media groups in order to compete with CCTV. Foreign programming is also available via satellite television.

A breakdown of China's audience rating figures is given in Appendix D.

SMG

The **Shanghai Media Group** (**SMG**) (Chinese: 上海文广新闻传媒集团) is a multimedia television and radio broadcasting, news and Internet company and is part of the Shanghai Media & Entertainment Group (SMEG). The company employs around 5,200 people, with capital assets totaling US$1.72 billion.

Formed in 2001, SMG's core business is television broadcasting and related media entertainment services including sports, showbiz, performance arts, science and technology, and finance. The television broadcasting media consist of 11 analogue TV channels, 90 digital cable pay-TV channels, a full broadcasting Internet TV service, along with 10 analogue and 19 digital radio services. The group also operates and owns five sports centers and 14 cultural art centers. Other areas of operation include newspapers, magazines, news websites, and audio-visual publishing.

According to an ACNielsen survey, 11 of the group's TV channels achieved a market share of 65% during prime time in 2008. Revenue from advertising accounts for about 10% of the commercial sales turnover in the local market. Being a producer and a publisher in the various fields of news, film, TV series, music, sports, finance, entertainment, and documentary, SMG is pushing itself towards the domestic and international Chinese-speaking market.

Through reinforcing financial initiatives, SMG is currently undergoing aggressive expansion into new areas such as cable pay TV services, program patent sales, brand-related business, and program innovation.

In January 2008, SMG launched an all-English channel, ICS (International Channel Shanghai), China's second 24-hour TV channel to broadcast nationwide in English.

China Central Television, Shanghai Media's biggest rival and controlled by the central government, also operates an English channel (CCTV-9) which targets a foreign audience, but of which the main audience is English-speaking local people.

Shanghai Media also aims to broadcast the planned English news channel to countries in Asia, Europe, and North America via satellite or through cooperation with local broadcasters.

BTV

China Beijing TV Station (Chinese: 北京电视台), a government-owned television network which broadcasts in the Chinese language from the nation's capital, has 10 primary channels. These include lifestyle and shopping channels, as well as the usual arts and entertainment, drama and sports channels.

Phoenix Satellite Television Holdings Ltd or **Phoenix Television** (Simplified Chinese: 凤凰卫星电视) is a Hong Kong-based Mandarin Chinese television broadcaster that serves the Chinese mainland and other markets with substantial numbers of Chinese viewers. Its five channels provide news, information and entertainment programs. The oldest of these channels, Phoenix Chinese Channel, began broadcasting in 1996 and now covers more than 42 million households and 150 million viewers in mainland China. It also reaches 53 countries and regions via satellite and has more than 20 million overseas viewers.

The company has enjoyed a good relationship with the Chinese government for many years and is one of the few privately owned broadcasting companies in mainland China able to broadcast information about events not covered by the government media. The company intends to move its corporate head office to Beijing.

Outdoor media

JCDecaux

Established in 1964, **JCDecaux** pioneered the street furniture concept and is today the leading outdoor advertising company in Europe and the Asia Pacific and is ranked second worldwide. Listed on the Euronext Paris, the Group owns 952,000 advertising panels in 54 countries and employs 8,900 people worldwide, generating total annual revenue of US$3 billion in 2007. JCDecaux China began operations in 2005 through acquiring reputable local outdoor advertising companies and other new contracts. The company's Chinese businesses now span 22 cities, including Hong Kong and Macau, creating the largest and most diversified outdoor-media network in Greater China, covering metro, bus, airport, street furniture and campus advertising.

Floating advertisements

On the Huangpu River in Shanghai's Bund area and on Canton's Zhujiang River, there is a new form of outdoor media: advertising boats on the river. These boats carry a huge double-sided LCD screen which runs advertising day and night and can be seen by potential consumers on both sides of the river.

Vega, the company that operates this business, offers a unique combination to luxury brands looking to create a presence in China. The Bund in Shanghai, in particular, offers a prestigious location in which to target an audience for top luxury brands. As we saw earlier, several such brands have already established a presence in Shanghai to take advantage of the fact that more than 200,000 Chinese executives work in the area and more than half-a-million people live in the nearby high-end residential areas. Add to these demographic advantages the number of visitors (more than 100,000 people visit the area monthly) and an established image of luxury, romance and enjoyment and floating advertising has the potential to work well for other luxury brands looking to enter the market.

Focus Media Group

Founded in 2003, the Focus Media Group provides a special advertising platform based mainly on LED in public places, such as lift lobbies, entertainment and social venues, shopping districts, mobile phones and residential complexes. It has some 112,000 flat-panel displays reaching higher-than-average-income individuals in over 90 cities in China.

Internet

With 298 million users, China now has the highest internet usage in the world, with numbers increasing at around 30% every year (33.8% in 2007 and 41.9% in 2008). At the end of 2008, 22.6% of the population were internet users, as opposed to an international average of 21.9%.[2] Details of internet distribution in different provinces are shown in Table 6.1.

TABLE 6.1: *Internet usage in China in 2007 and 2008, by province*

	End of 2007		End of 2008		
	Internet users (million)	Percentage of population	Internet users (million)	Percentage of population	Increase Rate 2007/2008
National	210	15.9%	298	22.6%	41.9%
Guangdong	33.44	35.9%	45.54	48.2%	36.2%
Zhejiang	15.09	30.3%	21.08	41.7%	39.7%
Jiangsu	17.57	23.3%	20.84	27.3%	18.6%
Shandong	12.56	13.5%	19.83	21.2%	57.9%
Fujian	8.66	24.3%	13.79	38.5%	59.3%
Hebei	7.62	11.1%	13.34	19.2%	75.0%
Henan	9.56	10.2%	12.83	13.7%	34.2%
Liaoning	7.83	18.3%	11.38	26.5%	45.3%
Shanghai	8.3	45.8%	11.1	59.7%	33.7%
Sichuan	8.09	9.9%	11.03	13.6%	36.4%
Hubei	7.06	12.4%	10.5	18.4%	48.7%
Hunan	6.9	10.9%	9.99	15.7%	44.7%
Beijing	7.37	46.6%	9.8	60.0%	32.9%
Shanxi	5.36	15.9%	8.19	24.1%	52.8%
Shaanxi	5.17	13.9%	7.9	21.1%	52.8%
Guangxi	5.6	11.9%	7.34	15.4%	31.1%
Anhui	5.87	9.6%	7.23	11.8%	23.1%
Xinjiang	3.63	17.7%	6.25	27.1%	72.1%
Heilongjiang	4.76	12.5%	6.2	16.2%	30.2%
Jiangxi	5.11	11.8%	6.1	14.0%	19.5%
Chongqing	3.56	12.7%	5.98	21.2%	67.9%
Yunnan	3.03	6.8%	5.48	12.1%	81.0%
Jilin	4.34	15.9%	5.2	19.0%	19.8%
Tianjin	2.87	26.7%	4.85	43.5%	69.1%
Guizhou	2.24	6.0%	4.33	11.5%	93.4%
Inner Mongolia	3.22	13.4%	3.85	16.0%	19.7%
Gansu	2.19	8.4%	3.27	12.5%	49.5%
Hainan	1.44	17.2%	2.16	25.6%	49.9%
Qinghai	0.6	11.0%	1.3	23.6%	117.4%
Ningxia	0.61	10.1%	1.02	16.6%	66.4%
Tibet	0.36	12.7%	0.47	16.4%	29.5%

Source: CNNIC 2008 Report

The rapid development of the internet in China has opened up a whole new range of target consumers, particularly young people, for mass-market products. Luxury brands, too, have begun to focus on the most influential portals (sohu.com and sina.com) and specialist websites (such as onlylady.com and rayli.com.cn) to communicate their brand message to a wider audience. Cosmetics and automobile brands were among the first luxury product categories to adopt this new medium as a tool of communication and branding.

Sohu.com

sohu.com is an internet media company providing Chinese consumers with a wide range of information, entertainment and communication options and wireless value-added services, such as news, music, and picture content sent via mobile phone. With these Chinese-language web navigational capabilities, Sohu provides brand advertising services in 35 main content channels, web-based communications and community services, and short messaging services. Each of its interest-specific main channels contains multi-level sub-channels that cover a range of topics, including news, business, entertainment and sports. Key features of the company's portal include navigational capabilities that reflect particular cultural characteristics and viewing habits of internet users in China.

Sina.com

sina.com is another online media company offering value-added information services in China and to Chinese communities worldwide. Through a network of localized websites its region-focused services include online news, search and enterprise services, mobile value-added services (MVAS) and online shopping.

Onlylady.com

onlylady.com is a portal catering to consumers in China's fashion and cosmetics industries. In 2007 it was acquired by CNET.com, a Nasdaq-listed interactive-media company. CNET.com operates two segments: U.S. Media and International Media. The former focuses on technology, entertainment, lifestyle and business. International

Media has similar coverage but also includes brands related to automotive and women's fashion represented in markets such as China. In January 2008, the Company acquired Cheshi.com, a Chinese automotive market website.

Rayli.com.cn

rayli.com.cn is the most important portal for the women's beauty and fashion industry in China. It offers a network of local Chinese websites and fashion magazines focusing on cosmetics, beauty tips, health and beauty hints, and a range of products for the modern Chinese woman. The company also operates a top model agency and a club for VIP fashion clients.

Celebrities and events

Celebrities from show business, sports or the business world are an established means for companies in the fashion and luxury industry to promote their brands. Their value comes from creating a positive association between the celebrity and the brand such that the key celebrity becomes associated with the brand's values. This can be used to great effect in China, too, as long as the image of the chosen celebrity is appropriate for the brand. While the desire to cash in on celebrity is one thing, it is important not to seek to do so at the expense of the brand's carefully developed image. The two do not always sit well together, as the following example shows.

In 2005, TAG Heuer launched a communication campaign in China using Yao Ming, the Chinese basketball player who is idolized by young sports-loving Chinese for his success in the NBA in the United States. However, people were confused by the brand positioning which saw a high-end Swiss-made watch matched with a famous basketball player because basketball is a mass-market sport, very popular among the young. TAG Heuer's usual target audience is more senior and whose sporting interests are tennis, golf or horse-riding— elegant sports with very strong upper-middle-class associations. The company overcame these image problems by recruiting international stars such as golf's superstar Tiger Woods and Formula One's Michael Schumacher who more closely matched the brand image.

The consistency of the brand's positioning vis-à-vis celebrity values is crucial. Simply putting a famous Chinese face on a brand is not going to work.

The image consistency problem of luxury brand communication in China does not stop here. There are other very serious image problems for Chinese movie stars that international brands often neglect. For example, the most famous Chinese international movie star, Gong Li, is considered by the international media to be the most beautiful Chinese woman in the world and has received lots of international awards. It would be very reasonable, you might think, to see her as the perfect ambassador for an international luxury brand in China. This was undoubtedly the reason behind Chopard's invitation to her to take part in advertising its luxury watches. Gong Li is undoubtedly beautiful and the photos were well designed to highlight the desired image of prestige and beauty. It was assumed that the desired information would be easily understood by the Chinese consumer, but this proved not to be the case.

The problem was that Chopard was not the only brand Gong Li represents. She also had advertising contracts with other international companies, such as L'Oréal, as well as with many Chinese companies in sectors ranging from local wines to motorcycles to refrigerators. The values Chopard wished to convey were confused by its star's association with other, mass-market, products.

If Chopard had used the marketing campaign only outside China, this may not have been such a problem. However, it chose to benefit from the high level of awareness the actress commanded without giving sufficient consideration to factors such as the attendant social, cultural, professional and economic background.

Chopard would have been well-advised to appoint a local marketing director to advise of the potential risks involved in using this Chinese star for an international luxury brand.

Another potential marketing communication problem for international luxury brands arises from differences between the product's concept and design environment, and the actual market environment.

For example, the information conveyed by the images used in the Giorgio Armani Spring/Summer advertising campaign for 2008 was very different from that used for Emporio Armani. The first used a post-modern approach designed for the European market. However, China is an emerging market not yet at the stage of full modernization and has very different values. The advertising failed to find resonance in China. Attempting to apply long-established luxury and fashion concepts developed in European countries will not work in China. The Emporio Armani advertising, however, was designed specifically for the Asian market and showed that the company had learned something of this by then. In choosing Jin Chengwu, the Taiwanese-Japanese movie star, and Zhang Ziyi, the Chinese movie star, to model its products, it managed to convey a completely different image—youth, good looks and success—to which Armani's target audience could more easily relate.

China is clearly in a relatively early stage of its social evolution; that is, modern, as opposed to Europe's post-modern development stage. The major differences between societies in different stages are summarized in Table 6.2. Such differences are evident across and between different geographic regions or countries, especially in emerging markets such as China, Brazil, Russia and India. The problems arising in this regard are less obvious for mass-market products and brands because of their universal functionality. But for luxury and fashion goods, the products and brands are the value vehicles which confront and conflict directly with the values of emerging markets such as China.

Countries still in the throes of the modernization process are characterized by a rapid increase in economic development. In China's case, this is evidenced by an average GDP growth rate of 9% over a period of 30 years, which stands in stark contrast to the near-zero rates recorded by many post-modern European societies. The process of modernization in China led to a fundamental questioning of the prevailing grand ideology and there was a great deal of discussion in the early stages of the opening and reform policy regarding the respective merits of communist and capitalist ideologies. This dilemma was resolved in Deng Xiaoping's now-famous phrase: "Be it a black cat or a white cat, a cat that can catch mice is a good cat." In other words, the most efficient way to develop the national economy is the right way. This had the effect of liberalizing the thinking of the Chinese people and gave the necessary social and political impetus for rapid economic development.

The contrasting dominant values of countries in the respective stages of development are outlined in Table 6.2. Countries in the post-modern stage have moved beyond the grand ideologies that mark the modernizing phase and tend to focus on the present, where the hedonistic pursuit of happiness and leisure dominate. In the modernizing phase currently being experienced in China, the consumer is looking for social success and accomplishment, and any good communication of luxury brands in China should emphasize personal success and its associated social goals.

TABLE 6.2: *Comparison of the different stages of social evolution*

	Modernism	Post-Modernism
Economic Environment	Rapid increase	Zero increase
Social Environment Dominant Values	Grand ideology: Capitalism, Marxism Cognition of future -development -work -reasons	Saturation of ideology Focus on present -suspicion -happiness and leisure -emotion
Personal	Social Success	Hedonistic

Source: Evrard, Pras and Roux, *Market, Etudes et Recherches en Marketing*, Dunod, Paris, 2000: 63

An example of how this can be achieved can be seen in recent changes employed by Mercedes in China. When the company, which has long been associated with prestige throughout the world and, indeed, in China, found that its image had become a little old and stale in the minds of Chinese consumers—and in the face of increased competition from the likes of Audi and BMW—in 2008 it launched an advertising and communication campaign to revitalize its brand image. Focusing on the young and newly wealthy in the private sector, it engaged Li Bingbing, a young female movie star (pictured below left), as an ambassador for its C-Class cars. It also sponsored a national concert tour for Li Biao (below right), the rising star musician who played drums at the closing ceremony of the Beijing Olympic Games.

Copyright: Fleishman-Hillard

In addition to differences in levels of social evolution, there are other important cultural differences between different cities and regions and their respective levels of brand awareness that need to be considered. The communication strategies available to luxury brands in this regard are summarized in Table 6.3.

The luxury brand's communication strategies should vary according to specific market circumstances. If its brand awareness is very high in a market which has a strong, established local culture (such as in China), the brand should integrate more local elements into its communications, much as Louis Vuitton did in using the Chinese supermodel Du Juan as the face of its international advertising campaign.

TABLE 6.3: *Adapting to cultural differences*

Local Market	Luxury Brand Awareness High	Luxury Brand Awareness Low
Local Culture: Strong	1. Integrate more local elements in brand's worldwide identity	3. Continue to build a strong brand with your international identity
Local Culture: Weak	2. Consider the local market as home country and standardize marketing communication	4. Start to build a strong brand with your international identity

Source: Pierre Xiao Lu, Elite China, Luxury Consumer Behavior in China, John Wiley & Sons, 2008: 185

A similar strategy was used to good effect by Omega which, as the official timekeeper and sponsor of the Beijing Olympics in 2008, took the opportunity to close the psychological gap between its luxury products and local Chinese consumers. It invited its world-wide ambassadors such as Nicole Kidman and Cindy Crawford to join various PR activities to promote various Chinese cultural activities. In doing so, it showed the kind of respect for Chinese culture that is crucial for doing business in China.

Another example of the kind of connection that can be forged in the minds of consumers can be seen in Blancpain's decision to associate its brand with Beijing's Forbidden City. In 2008, Blancpain developed the Qianlong watch for the Forbidden City's haute horology collection, and is the only modern watch in the collection. Qianlong, the sixth emperor of the Qing dynasty, was born in 1735—the year of Blancpain's foundation in Switzerland. The unique watch was created as a celebration of these events and draws them together in a perfect combination for successful brand communication in China.

Another luxury-watch maker, Breguet, also sponsored an exhibition from the Louvre Museum in Paris in the Forbidden City's Palace Museum in 2008. The exhibition presented three models of Breguet watches used by Napoleon Bonaparte at different periods of his life. To the Chinese, Napoleon is an almost-mythological revolutionary leader who was responsible for destroying the European feudal system. In associating its luxury products with such a symbol of power and success and, at the same time, with a top-level cultural

Nicole Kidman participated in Omega's PR activities with Chinese minorities on the Bund in Shanghai 2008
Copyright: Fleishman-Hillard

exchange linking the Louvre with the Forbidden City, Breguet positioned itself perfectly with both Chinese luxury consumers and specialist watch collectors.

Michelle Chen, marketing and communication director of Ports 1961, believes that success in organizing fashion and luxury PR events in China depends on being able to find interesting and attractive themes that match well with the current socioeconomic development. For example, in 2006, Ports sponsored the apparel featured in the successful Hollywood movie "The Devil Wears Prada," and hosted the Premiere Party for the movie in Beijing. These marketing activities had the effect of linking the company with Hollywood stars in the minds of Chinese consumers.

Breguet and Blancpain organized PR activity in the Forbidden City, 2008
Copyright: Fleishman-Hillard

In addition to general marketing communications, in-store events are extremely effective in helping to retain established customers and VIP clients. Brands such as Zegna, Louis Vuitton, Cartier and many others have adopted this method, organizing such things as in-store shows or afternoon tea for clients to maintain and stimulate their interest. Lacoste took this a step further in 2008 when it combined its sponsorship of the international Tennis Masters Cup in Shanghai with in-store promotional events

Ports 1961 fashion show at the premiere of "The Devil Wears Prada" in China
Copyright: Ports 1961

Lacoste in-store event in Raffles City during the Tennis Masters Cup, Shanghai, 2008
Copyright: Xu Wen

to celebrate the brand's 75th anniversary. A huge exhibition and boutique in the form of a tennis court was built in the central hall of Raffles City—the trendiest shopping mall for teenagers and young people—in downtown People's Square, next door to Nanjing East Road, the liveliest commercial street in the world.

Communication models for advertising luxury brands

Luxury brands are in the business of dealing with cultural and artistic attitudes and values, elements of which they have to keep in mind in a new cultural environment such as China. In this regard, set out below are three basic but very effective communication models for luxury brands advertising in China: the means-ends chain theory;[3] the meaning movement and endorsement process;[4] and the advertising planning model.[5]

The means-ends chain

Means-ends chain theory was developed in the 1980s as a tool linking consumers' knowledge of product characteristics and their own needs in the consumer decision-making process.

The means-end chain models, as illustrated in Figure 6.1, is a conceptual tool which allows a better understanding of how consumers perceive the self-relevant outcomes of product use and consumption.

This model links consumer and product together by building an associative network between concrete and abstract product attributes, functional and psychosocial consequences with product use and consumers' instrumental and terminal values.[6] Product attributes are the means through which consumers achieve their ultimate values/ends, via the positive consequences or benefits accruing from the attributes. In other words, goods/services are seen as a means to satisfy needs that are conscious to varying degrees.

FIGURE 6.1: *The means-end chain model*

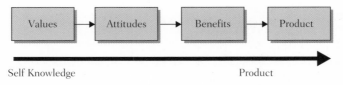

Source: Gutman, J. 1982

In this means-ends chain model, products are not chosen and purchased for themselves or their characteristics, but for the meaning they engender in the mind of the buyer. In this way products, though selected for fairly concrete features such as their characteristics and attributes (color, shape, size, origin, and so on), and for the benefits which they are capable of providing—functional or psychosocial consequences (for example, a fashionable look; a healthy and tasty diet)—are in fact perceived subconsciously as aimed at and connected with the achievement of individual goals. In the case of luxury goods, the carriers of strong values and attitudes, the product attributes with functional and psychosocial meanings reflect more directly the consumers' individual goals, which may be to display wealth, social status and personal tastes.

A means-ends chain is a conceptual structure linking a product and a consumer. Attributes of products are assumed to lead to various consequences of product use or consumption, which in turn satisfy consumers' values. When cultural background changes, the consumers' values change as well; thus whether the attributes of a product can satisfy consumers' needs becomes problematic, especially for high-involvement products such as luxury goods. The means-ends chain model would look very different from the perspective of the Chinese consumer from the way it might look to the luxury brand's designer, as illustrated in Figure 6.2.

FIGURE 6.2: *Different perspectives of the means-ends chain*

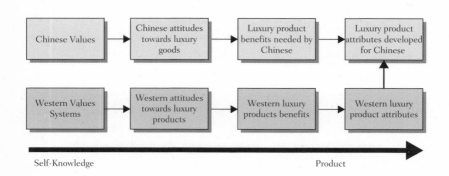

The problem for international luxury brands in China is how to let Chinese consumers accept psychologically a product with attributes and values developed and based on a Western cultural background. While this is not easy, it can be achieved, as the examples outlined above clearly show.

Meaning movement and the endorsement process (How to use celebrities)

Advertisers must try to match the product/company image, the characteristics of the target market, and the personality of the celebrity they choose to represent them. The celebrity's image projected to consumers can be just as important as their ability to attract attention. Grant McCracken developed a perspective on the celebrity-endorsement process and argued that credibility and attractiveness don't sufficiently explain how and why celebrity endorsements work, and offered a model based on meaning transfer, as shown in Figure 6.3.

According to this model, a celebrity's effectiveness as an endorser depends on the culturally acquired meanings he or she brings to the endorsement process. Each celebrity contains many meanings, including status, class, gender and age, as well as personality and lifestyle. McCracken pointed out that celebrities draw powerful meanings from the roles they assume in their television, movie, military, athletic, and other careers. Each new dramatic role brings the celebrity into contact with a range of objects, persons, and contexts which transfer meanings which then come to reside in the celebrity. In the second stage, celebrity endorsers bring their meanings and image into the ad and transfer them to the product they are endorsing. In the final stage, the meanings the celebrity gives to the product are transferred to the consumer.

While using local celebrities is an effective way of resolving cultural conflicts in the means-end chain and of closing the psychological distance between Western luxury goods and Chinese luxury consumers, the real challenge lies in choosing the appropriate stars, as we saw earlier.

FIGURE 6.3: *McCracken's meaning-transfer model*

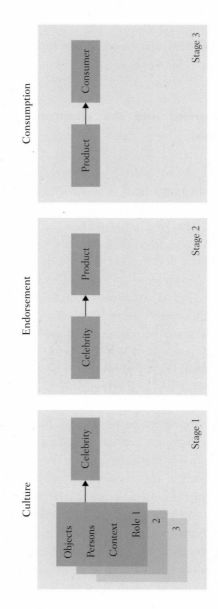

Source: McCracken 1989

Examples of the successful use of celebrity image by luxury brands in China include Montblanc's signing up of the young pianist Lang Lang to be its worldwide brand ambassador. It has also made intelligent use of Cui Jian, the founder of Chinese rock and pop music, at its PR events, linking its luxury products to the idol of the young people of the 1980s and '90s who are some of today's most successful business people.

Chinese rock star Cui Jian at Montblanc store opening, Beijing, 2008
Copyright: Fleishman-Hillard

While Jaeger-LeCoultre has a very high-end masculine image for Chinese businessmen and CEOs, it also has very beautiful product lines for women, which it has promoted at PR events and boutique openings through Taiwanese movie star Shu Qi, whose fresh, fashionable image epitomizes the qualities the brand wishes to convey to its targeted consumers.

In 2009, Omega signed Zhang Ziyi, star of such film's as Ang Lee's "Crouching Tiger, Hidden Dragon," Zhang Yimou's "Hero" and

Shu Qi with Jaeger-LeCoultre watch
Copyright: Fleishman-Hillard

"The Road Home," Wong Karwai's "2046" and Jackie Chan's "Rush Hour 2," as its international ambassador. She is also the ambassador for Mercedes' SLK Passion 08 Roadster, which matches well with Omega's high-end positioning and image in the market. Here, there is none of the brand confusion and mixed messages discussed earlier.

Advertising planning model

The advertising planning model was developed by Richard Vaughn and his associates in the Foote, Cone and Belding advertising agency 30 years ago. The model was based on the hierarchy-of-effects model and its variants and research on high and low involvement,

Zhang Ziyi, Omega's international ambassador in 2009
Copyright: Fleishman-Hillard

and brain specialization in thinking-versus-feeling processing. It delineates four primary advertising planning strategies—informative, affective, habit formation, and satisfaction—along with the most appropriate variant of the alternative response hierarchies.

Four models are classified and adapted to the luxury and fashion goods environment in Table 6.4. Luxury and fashion goods are high-involvement products. But their characteristics are different according to different product categories. For example, luxury cars, villas, complicated watches and high-end high-tech products have some technical aspects for consumers to learn and perhaps study. Thus it needs more analytical thinking from consumers to learn about the product and brand, before involving their emotions and feelings into the decision-making process. But with fashion and cosmetic products, the emotion and feeling works *before* the analytical thinking about the technical aspects of the product. However, communication that logically focuses on some special technical aspects supporting the exclusivity and high-end positioning could have the effect of distancing consumers. The perfect communication strategy is one which combines the analytical with the emotional.

TABLE 6.4: *Vaughn's model adapted to luxury and fashion-goods advertising planning*

	Thinking	Feeling
High Involvement: Luxury Product	1. Informative Luxury Car – Villas and High-end house – High Tech– new products Model: Learn – feel – do	2. Affective Jewelry – cosmetics – fashion apparel Model: Feel – learn – do
Low Involvement: Mass-Market Product	3. Habit formation Food – household items Model: Do – learn – feel	4. Self-satisfaction Cigarettes – liquor – candy Model: Do – feel – learn

Source: Belch & Belch, Advertising and Promotion, McGraw-Hill, Sixth Edition, 2004

In the case of affective luxury product categories, the emphasis is on the emotional side of the brand, especially for fashion products: consumers are firstly attracted by the feeling they get from the brand image and the product, and then go into the store for more information.

For some years, Mercedes-Benz has had a brand problem in China because in the minds of the wealthy young it had become associated with the over-fifties age group. In an attempt to change this view, in 2008 Mercedes invited Zhang Ziyi to endorse its CLS class sports car. Through a clever interplay of language in the advertising slogans such that the "extreme beauty" of the CLS and that of its endorser become intertwined, the company has been able to establish the brand's attractiveness and create the necessary affective and emotional attachment among younger consumers.

The problem for a secondary fashion brand is to ensure that the brand image, as it is perceived by the potential consumer, really embodies the brand's values and symbolic meanings. In this regard,

Zhang Ziyi's advertising for Mercedes-Benz CLS, Hangzhou Airport, 2009
Copyright: Fleishman-Hillard

in-store merchandising and visual displays are very important aspects of brand communication. Zara's communication strategy worldwide is based entirely on its huge stores, which are all situated in the most strategic location of luxury and fashion districts. This is also the case with the company's first flagship store in Shanghai, which is strategically positioned on Nanjing West Road facing Plaza 66, the city's luxury landmark.

But many local fashion and luxury operators in China have failed to consider this point in their branding strategies, preferring to open up in less-visible locations in secondary shopping malls as a way of lowering their costs. This has the effect of tarnishing the brand image and making it less attractive to high-end consumers. This is a situation that luxury brands have to avoid when it comes to choosing business partners (agents and distributors) in China. The best solution is to choose a big distributor with an established portfolio of international brands in the market and strong financial support. To estimate the future effect of the brand image, it pays to visit all stores (in first-tier and secondary cities, premium and secondary location stores) of other brands for which it acts as distributor in order to evaluate its performance and to establish a benchmark for strategic decision-making.

ENDNOTES

1   See Doctoroff 2005: 141.
2   Source: http://www.internetworldstats.com
3   Gutman 1982: 60–72.
4   McCracken 1989.
5   Vaughn 1980: 27.
6   Rokeach 1973.

The War of the Spirits

The alcohol culture in China

China has 1.3 billion people and is the world's leading market for beer (380 million ml production)[1] and spirits (4.93 million tons of production). China has a very long history of alcohol consumption, almost as long as its history, in fact. However, the consumption culture is very different from that in the United States or Europe.

The Chinese spirits market is a unique and independent market outside of the global wine and spirits market, because Chinese spirits (*baijiu*) are white liquor based on rice or sorghum, which is different from the "brown" products, such as whisky and cognac or the "white" products, such as vodka and rum.

Though often mistakenly referred to as "wine" or "white wine," *baijiu*, which translates as "white liquor," "white alcohol" or "white spirits," is actually a distilled liquor, generally about 80–120° proof, or 40–60% alcohol by volume (ABV) (ethanol). It is usually distilled from sorghum, although in southern China it is typically made from glutinous rice, and in northern China it can also be made from wheat, barley or millet. Because of its clarity, *baijiu* can appear similar to several other liquors, but generally has a significantly higher ABV than, say, vodka (35–50%), Japanese *shōchū* (25%), or Korean *soju* (20–45%), and a flavor that is distinctive and unique.

Baijiu is generally sold in glass or ceramic bottles and consumed in shot-glasses, much like vodka. It is traditional to consume *baijiu* with food rather than on its own, though the latter is not uncommon. *Baijiu* can be integrated into cocktails as well.[2]

Imported products are generally perceived to be better, more "cultured," than their local counterparts. Drinking imported liquor is seen to signify affluence and sophistication. However, given their relatively recent exposure to foreign liquor, Chinese consumers have difficulty differentiating the taste of whisky from cognac and little knowledge of the traditions surrounding the drinking of cognac as a *digestif*, for example. As a result, the Chinese often drink cognac throughout a meal. To compound these problems, the wine-and-spirits market is overflowing with counterfeit versions, further crippling the Chinese ability to differentiate.

The main competitors

Since China joined the World Trade Organization, the embargo on the trade of foreign wines has been lifted and the tax rate on has been reduced from 19.2% to 10%.

There are three main players in China's spirits market: Chivas (Pernod Ricard), Johnnie Walker (Diageo), and Hennessy (LVMH). Other direct (imported) competitors include Royal Salute, Remy Martin, Glenfiddich (pure malt), Glenfarclas (pure malt), Ballentine's, Dewar's, Jack Daniel's, J&B, Famous Grouse, Matisse, Jim Beam, and Suntory. Local competition comes from China's white liquor: Mao Tai and Wu Liang Ye (each has a 30% share of the high-end white-liquor market).

Chivas: Established in Scotland in 1801, the company has a long history of distilling to exceptionally high standards. Now controlled by Pernod Ricard, Chivas entered the Chinese market in 1992. Its product range comprises:

- Chivas 12, the entry-point "core brand" which focuses on new and emerging markets;
- Chivas 18, a "driver brand" designed for those looking for a more intense and sophisticated whisky experience; and

Chinese white liquor "Mao Tai" and "Wu Liang Ye"
Copyright: Xu Wen

- Chivas 25, the "halo brand," which is seen as the ultimate expression of the Chivas Regal style and designed for the most discerning of drinkers.

Johnnie Walker: In 2001, Johnnie Walker—established in Scotland in 1820 and now owned by Diageo, the largest multinational beer, wine and spirits company—became widely available in China, boasting record global annual sales of 4.5 million nine-liter cases in 2008.

Hennessy: Having moved to France from Ireland in 1745, Richard Hennessy established his own wine factory in 1765 and, over eight successive generations, the family company became a byword for cognac in far-flung corners of the world, including Japan in 1868 and Shanghai in 1872. In 1971, Hennessy went into partnership with Moët & Chandon, making Moët-Hennessy, today a division of the LVMH group, one of the world's largest wine-and-spirit structures.

Distribution

Spirits are widely distributed through pubs, where fashion shows are held and ideas are exchanged, and KTV lounges. KTV, a variant of karaoke, is one of the most popular night-time activities for young people in China. A typical KTV establishment contains 10–20 private rooms containing karaoke equipment rented out to small groups. These rooms can be extremely opulent and alcohol helps fuel the entertainment.

While hotels and restaurants continue to serve spirits to their customers, they are facing strong competition from beers and Chinese white liquor. In general, spirits companies do not see hotels and restaurants as a major volume channel, but they see it as necessary to maintain a good relationship with these establishments.

Increasingly, the famous whisky brands can be found in supermarkets and convenience stores. As purchasing power rises and prices fall, whisky has become a lot more widely available for family gatherings. Imported varieties are also becoming the gift of choice while visiting friends and relatives during traditional festivals.

Marketing strategies

In China, the consumption culture for alcohol is radically different from other parts of the world. David Hunt, president of Tequila PR which manages marketing strategy for Chivas in China, sees the main consumer group as "youngsters above 25 years old who are open-minded, willing to accept new ideas and brands." Arguably, they buy Chivas not because of their discerning taste in alcohol consumption but because it's expensive. Nowadays, more than 70% of the sales volume comes from night venues, compared with 30% in Taiwan. In 2004 (the latest date for which information is currently available), whisky sales in China increased by 170%, compared to the global worldwide sales increase of 2%. And from 1999 to 2004, the consumption of whisky in China increased 296%.

During the summer of 2005, a gentleman dressed exactly like the man in the Johnnie Walker logo appeared in the nightclubs of Shanghai, Guangzhou, Beijing, Shenzhen and other big cities to promote the brand and was quickly accepted by consumers. Through the campaign, the company easily reached its target consumers and brought about a rapid increase in brand awareness.

Having entered the Chinese market very early through Hong Kong, Hennessy has been able to establish a very exclusive brand image, creating different positioning for its product range. The range includes, for example, V.S.O.P. Privilege—with the slogan "Live a fantasy life"—which is a lower-end sub-brand aimed at those who cannot afford Hennessy's more expensive products but who aspire to become part of the exclusive group who can.

Hennessy X.O. has become a symbol of luxury. It is seen as a reflection of the success and leadership qualities of those who own (but who don't necessarily drink) it. Indeed, X.O. is as much for collecting as it is for drinking. At the next level, there is Private Reserve, with a numbered code on each bottle. This is for the true connoisseur, one who appreciates the product for itself rather than as a social status symbol.

Advertising and sponsorship

Most television advertising campaigns employed by the wines-and-spirits companies in China make use of celebrities. Chivas ads usually feature a backdrop of the great outdoors—usually an enchanting locale that beckons the viewer to escape into the Chivas fantasy. One, roughly translated "Fishing in a World of Ice and Snow," had such a catchy background tune that a large audience asked to download it from the internet. Another recent ad featured the high-end Chivas Regal 18 (which has a gold lion on the label as a symbol of social status).

The company has also used several humorous print ads designed both to educate the drinker and to emphasize its credentials as a responsible member of society.

Copyright: Pernod Ricard

Hennessy's TV advertisements, which focus mainly on the low-end V.S.O.P., highlight its "Live in fantasy" message and the slogan "That's what I am." All of its print ads present people (actors) delighting in the natural world against a backdrop of the setting sun, or on a pristine beach or simply in the silence of the night.

In 2009, Chivas launched its "Live with Chivalry" international advertising campaign for Chivas Regal, promoting a positive view of life. The campaign, inspired by the timeless values of chivalry, is aimed at "modern knights," encouraging us to live life with honor, loyalty, camaraderie and gallantry.

The four print ads and two TV commercials were commissioned following international research which showed that the values associated with chivalry are almost universally attractive in today's society.

"Live with Chivalry": Chivas Global Advertising Campaign 2009
Copyright: Pernod Ricard

In addition to advertisements, event sponsorships have also helped to significantly promote each brand. In July 2008, for example, Chivas sponsored a Black Eyed Peas concert. Johnnie Walker has sponsored F1's McLaren Team since 2005, its logo appearing on the car and the team uniform. It also sponsors the Johnnie Walker Classic Golf campaign.

Hennessy sponsored the Shen Zhen Ace Personal Collection Exhibition, which was named after the cognac. Hennessy City Cocktails, however, is by far the most popular event, held in four cities around the world: Paris, Moscow, Miami and Shanghai.

The greatest obstacle facing those who want to enter the Chinese luxury spirits market remains the need to educate Chinese consumers about the different tastes from different brands. Running a close second, however, is the problem of counterfeiting (as it affects the luxury industry as a whole). To illustrate this, just a few days before the Lunar New Year in 2006 *International Finance* magazine ran an article about fake Chivas Regal 12 on the market. Despite the company's best efforts to set the record straight, 73.6% of customers were still unwilling to buy Chivas.

Major issues

One striking aspect of this brand war in China is that the best-selling products seem to be those that are trendiest and present the most amusement at nightclubs.

As they become "lifestyle brands," the major wines-and-spirits brands are competing head on and are differentiating themselves from their competitors on the basis of brand identity, their color codes, their aesthetic values and their public relations activities.

Behind all this, of course, there are long histories of product and brand development, family care and product selection in a sophisticated environment. The question is whether it is necessary to communicate this to the Chinese consumer, to train the consumer to classify different products, understand their origin and be attentive to what makes each of them special and different.

In a way, the alternative here is a trade-off between brand power and brand identity.

A second issue relates to the type of distribution better adapted to the growth of the product category and to the development of individual brands. Today, the market is split between nightclub and restaurant sales on the one side, and supermarket sales—where products are purchased for gifts and home consumption—on the other. It seems that nightclub activities create awareness among the young and that most of the major brands have concentrated their promotional efforts on what people call "on-premises" consumption.

But is there another way? Can a brand develop its sales on the basis of "off-premises" activities, such as sales in supermarkets? This would obviously require a different marketing approach, one which concentrates on a "pull" strategy (in contrast with a push strategy in nightclubs) and the education of the consumer on the specific qualities of a product that make it different from another.

Given the reality that the most powerful brands must be sold both "off" and "on" premises, and that success in one area does not necessarily translate into success in the other, this issue is not easily resolved.

Another, related, issue concerns the major thrust of the communication program. Should the emphasis be on television and outdoor advertising or should major PR activities be focused on nightclubs and restaurants? While the latter has the advantage of being workable within a limited budget, if the idea is to convince consumers to buy a given brand of whisky in the supermarkets, television advertising is probably the more effective approach to take.

Each brand must define for itself a mix that works, and this will be different for each. The trick lies in finding the most effective means at different times of the product's penetration in the Chinese market. There is no simple formula for this.

The international brands may find that a completely different approach is called for in the Chinese market. Wines such as Dynasty or Great Wall have demonstrated that extensive advertising activities are not always necessary. These products have been developed quite successfully through word of mouth and a presence on supermarket shelves. Could spirits also develop away from the nightclubs and by a sheer presence in supermarkets?

The best strategy for international spirits company to benefit from the huge Chinese white-liquor market lies not in trying to change the taste of Chinese drinkers, but to be Chinese. That is what Diageo and LVMH are trying to do. Diageo acquired the Shui Jing Fang brand in 2007; LVMH bought the Wen Jun brand in Sichuan province; and Pernod Ricard established a joint venture with the Jian Nan Chun group in Sichuan to produce high-end white liquor under Jian Nan Chun's name. But with the Chinese Anti Trust Law delivered in 2008, it will be difficult for international brands to take over new Chinese star brands in different fields. For example, Coca-Cola's attempt to purchase Chinese Huiyuan Juice was rejected by the Chinese Ministry of Commerce in March 2009.

ENDNOTES

1   China Food Industry Association, 2007.

2   Benjamin Siegel, "Make mine a baijiu, Bartender," *Time,* July 23, 2007.

CHAPTER 7

Brand Protection and Counterfeit Activities

Counterfeit activities in China

E VERYTHING today, from cognac to mineral water, can be, and very often is, counterfeited. Luxury is one of the most popular sectors for counterfeiters, because it is cheap to copy and easy to sell. In 2000, the Global Anti-Counterfeiting Group reported that 11% of the world's clothing and footwear was fake, and the World Customs Organization believes that the fashion industry loses up to US$9.2 billion per year to counterfeiting. In 2004, the European Commission reported that trade in counterfeit clothing, footwear, perfume and toiletries reduced the European Union's gross domestic product by more than US$6 billion each year and cost 10,800 jobs, with the figures increasing every year.

More than 80% of fake luxury products come from Asia, especially from China. But the counterfeit business chain is worldwide. It has the potential to be even more profitable than drug trafficking but is much less risky because it is considered to be a minor crime. For some brands, the number of counterfeits on the market may exceed the number of original pieces. The development of new technologies, especially the proliferation of the internet, allows counterfeit activities to extend to the virtual world and into the homes of billions of internet users. It is very difficult to track the source of such activities and the counterfeiters very often operate from countries which have weak law enforcement regarding cyber criminality.

In the book *Deluxe*, Dana Thomas outlines the development of this illegal industry, from humble beginnings in the 1970s and

1980s when the quality of the products—generally sold by merchants on the street—was very poor and prices were very cheap. This presented no real threat to the luxury brands, but with the democratization of luxury through the media and new technologies created a huge potential international market. At the same time, the opening up of China in the 1980s meant that China became the world's factory for labor-intensive industries, such as textiles and light industrial products, enabling high productivity for low-cost products. Fashion goods provide the perfect business model for counterfeiting: they offer famous brands and expensive goods that everybody wants; they are easy and cheap to copy; the final results are very easy to sell; and the market is worldwide. In addition, the consequences for the counterfeiters if they are caught (which is very difficult in itself) are fairly minor. Even in the U.S., 99% of those caught in New York State do not go to jail. The crime is seen as being equivalent to stealing a car.

Louis Vuitton, the most copied and counterfeited luxury brand, employs 40 in-house lawyers and 250 outside investigators to counter these activities. It invests around US$18 million every year fighting against counterfeiting around the world.

Even though most counterfeited goods are manufactured in China, people here still fight against counterfeiting. In 2006, five high-fashion brands, Burberry, Chanel, Gucci, Prada and Louis Vuitton, won a lawsuit against the Xiushui (Silk) Market in the Civil Tribunal of Beijing. That same year, Lacoste and the Silk Market signed an agreement under which the Silk Market guaranteed that no fake Lacoste products would be sold in the market; and another market notorious for selling counterfeit products, the Shanghai Xiangyang market, was closed down.

Even though both governments and the luxury brands themselves may make great efforts to fight against counterfeiting, such activities show no sign of letting up and, indeed, have introduced many new trends in counterfeit luxury goods. These include quality improvements and more sophisticated distribution channels. It used to be the case that, in general, the quality of counterfeit products was obviously inferior to the original. However, with developments in technology and greater skills among their workers in China, counterfeit factories can now manufacture high-quality apparel, perfumes, cosmetics, leather goods, alcohol, watches, and so on. These are then distributed in much more organized and less-visible ways in non-commercial districts.

Visitors to Plaza 66 or the Bund in Shanghai or to the Guomao district in Beijing are frequently confronted by sellers of counterfeit goods displaying their wares directly outside the genuine luxury stores. The fact that they find it profitable to appear in such places is a clear indication that their customers more than likely include potential buyers of genuine luxury goods.[1]

Canadian journalist Naomi Klein's book *No Logo* (published in 2000 and subtitled "Taking Aim at the Brand Bullies") captures the mood of antagonism towards branding and has become part of a wider groundswell against globalization. Brand names such as Nike or Pepsi have expanded beyond the products which bore those names to become associated with everything from movie stars and athletes to grassroots social movements. The large multinational corporations, say their critics, consider the marketing of a brand name to be more important than the actual manufacture of products. Thus, many more people are likely to express their discontent by buying counterfeit goods as a way of undermining the established brands.

People throughout Europe and North America are increasingly suspicious of the motivations of the brands, are tired of materialism and commercial propaganda and want to return to the basic product level and to a more natural and ecologically sound way of living. However, for reasons explained in the previous chapter, this movement cannot find a mass audience in emerging countries such as China which are still in the process of modernization. The domestic market still remains dynamic and anti-branding or anti-globalization sentiments barely exist in the general public.

Where a rebellious attitude against luxury brands does exist, this is more than likely born of high prices and a perception of arrogance on the part of international luxury brands towards their Chinese consumers. The arrogant attitude experienced by Chinese consumers often comes from the sales staff in the luxury stores, which presents a challenge to the brands to train their staff in how to behave appropriately. They should be aware that Chinese consumers are generally unfamiliar with the business of luxury brands and, until they gain familiarity, may feel a psychological distance when they enter a store. The fact that they enter, even though they may feel out of place, is an indication that they are interested in knowing more; but if they are not made to feel comfortable, they are likely to form strong feelings against the brand in question and are unlikely ever to return. Sales staff have to be trained to be more sensitive to a potential client's feelings and not to make judgments about them based on the clothes or jewelry they are wearing or what handbag they are carrying. A good impression created on first contact can be much more efficient in communicating the brand message than any campaign in the press.

The mentality of copying

The fight against counterfeiting is made more difficult by the fact that China does not have a history of intellectual-property ownership. In fact, copying has been one of the cornerstones of its cultural history. Confucius was the first to democratize education, and he encouraged the copying of the works of great scholars as a means of spreading knowledge. In more recent times, China's Communist leaders declared that the State, rather than individuals, companies or corporations, owned all property. The first patent and trademark laws were not enacted until the early 1980s and these created a real dilemma in a culture where there is a very strong heritage of copying. The process of learning the Chinese language is also a process of copying as a means of memorizing several thousand characters. Indeed, to the Chinese mentality, learning and copying are almost synonymous. If something is admired and worth learning from, this leads naturally to the action of copying.

Copying has always been an accepted learning procedure and copying artistic masterpieces was a normal learning process. In fact, some of the most precious pieces of Chinese calligraphy in the National Museum in Beijing are, in fact, copies of the "Lan Ting Xu" (Preface to the Poems Composed at the Orchid Pavilion) by Wang Xizhi (303–361, Jin Dynasty), the most-revered of all Chinese calligraphers.[2] The copies include the following, by the Renzong emperor of the Song Dynasty, and Mao Zedong, the former president of China.

Zhao Zhen (赵桢, 1010–63), Renzong Emperor of Song Dynasty (960–1279)
Copyright: Pierre Xiao Lu

Mao Zedong (毛泽东, 1893–1976), President of People's Republic of China (1949–76)
Copyright: Pierre Xiao Lu

Brand protection in China

Given Chinese attitudes towards copying and the practical difficulties involved in countering counterfeit activities, all brands—international and local alike—face considerable challenges in protecting their brand image. Lawsuits are costly and can often outweigh the benefits of winning. But there are things that brands can do by way of protecting their interests.

Brand registration

A brand consists of a name and a company trademark. China amended its Trademark Law in line with international standards after its accession to the WTO in 2001.

Of particular importance for luxury brands is the fact that, in 2003, the concept of well-known marks and the process of applying for "well-known" status were clarified by the regulations for the Recognition and Protection of Well Known Marks under the Paris Convention. The "well-known trademark" status is very useful, especially for luxury brands, for which brand awareness is one of the most important brand assets.

However, this status is very difficult to obtain and requires substantial evidence to establish that the brand is famous in its country of origin as well as globally, and proof of its substantial use in China. As at the end of 2008, a total 1,189 Chinese trademarks had been confirmed as well-known in China and 102 international trademarks had been recognized (see Appendix E). Of the latter, however, only 23 (including five Hong Kong and Taiwanese brands) are high-end brands. These comprise seven watch and jewelry brands—Cartier, Tissot, Tudor, Rolex, De Beers, Chow Tai Fook, Chow Tai Seng; six cosmetic brands (with three belonging to the L'Oréal group)—Lancôme, Maybelline, L'Oréal; and Natural Beauty, Orlane and Avon; five fashion brands—Montagut, Yves Saint Laurent, Ports, Goldlion, and Boss; four high-end automobile brands—Ferrari, Jaguar, Porsche, and Lexus; and one hotel chain brand—Shangri-la.

Of the 23 high-end brands listed, only 13 are international luxury brands in the traditional luxury business field. Many of the most prestigious international luxury brands—including Chanel, Christian Dior, Hermès, Louis Vuitton, Prada and Gucci—are not in the current list, which means that if their products are copied or their brands are registered by others in other product categories, they cannot invoke the "well-known trademark" clause to protect themselves. This is why the luxury brands are subject to so much counterfeiting. The luxury brands themselves need to do more in this regard.

Fake "dunhill" and "Playboy" stores along a Shanghai street, 2009
Copyright: Pierre Xiao Lu

If they have an established presence in China, such as a representative office, foreign companies can start the procedure directly with the Trademark Office. Alternatively, they can obtain trademark rights through a designated trademark agent accepted and registered with the Trademark Office. Care is required, though, because there are hundreds of trademark agencies of variable quality and making the wrong choice can be costly of time, energy and money. The most reputable IP law firm in China is Wanhuida in Beijing, which helped Lacoste in its fight against counterfeiters, the most successful case in international luxury-brand protection in China.

Curbing counterfeiting

Like poverty and luxury, the counterfeit is inevitable in a commercial society. It has to be lived with but fought against with all possible means. Particularly in China, the only effective way to ensure protection of the brand is for the brand owner to take action. This may be difficult but it is not impossible, as the experience of the Richemont, Swatch and L'Oréal groups has shown.

There are two main formal possibilities to fight against counterfeiting activities: by administrative action or through the People's Courts. The advantage of the former is that it accepts a lower threshold of evidence and is the fastest way to take action to stop the counterfeit activities.

Administrative action

There are several administrative authorities with responsibility for protecting different areas of intellectual property rights, as set out in Table 7.1.

TABLE 7.1: *China's fight against counterfeiters*[3]

Authority	IP right
Administration for Industry and Commerce (AIC)	Trademarks Unfair-competition actions Trade
Technical Supervision Bureau (TSB)	Labeling, advertising, anti-counterfeiting, product-quality issues
Intellectual Property Offices	Patents (including design patents)
National Copyright Administration	Copyright

Source: Ordish and Adcock

But the authorities will take action only in cases where there is a direct copy of a copyright work, rather than focusing on whether a substantial part of the work has been copied. This means that in order to start the enforcement procedure, it is necessary to collect as much evidence as possible to prove that the brand and product has been massively copied in some concrete locations. For many brands familiar with the European or American legal environment, this may seem like an impossible task and they may think that it should be the job of the government, to whom they pay taxes, to protect their intellectual-property rights. But in China, except in cases where the infringed goods pose a public health or safety threat, the authorities take a more passive role in investigating infringements and do so only at the request of brand owners.

In this regard, Lexus, for example, appoints investigating companies to investigate specific activities or follow up on allegations of possible counterfeiting. If there is sufficient evidence to support such claims, the company's legal department then lodges an official complaint with the local authorities. Perhaps because auto parts have an important bearing on people's lives and safety, the State attaches a great deal of importance to these complaints and Lexus has yet to register a complaint that hasn't been settled. If necessary, where Lexus cannot obtain satisfaction from the relevant local authorities, it is prepared to take its case to higher levels and even as far as the central government, where complaints lodged by Lexus and other organizations are taken up by Japanese government bodies such as the Japan External Trade Organization, and the Quality Brands Protection Committee. Japan also has recourse to the International Intellectual Property Protection Forum (IIPPF), established for governmental and non-governmental entities in 2002, enabling it to crack down on the selling of counterfeit Japanese products in other countries.

Civil litigation

Taking action against counterfeiters through the courts is the only way of ensuring a direct impact on the counterfeiters' interests and stopping their activities. The case brought against the silk market in Beijing and the mediation between Lacoste and the silk market are good examples of what can be achieved.

For any action to succeed, either through the courts or through administrative procedures, the documentary evidence required must be strong and unchallengeable. It might include such things as original advertisements and promotional materials, photos of promotions and billboards, product samples and catalogues, invoices of marketing spend, trade fair materials and websites, details of global and Chinese trademarks, patents and copyrights, partnership and licensing agreements, and so on.

Working directly with the Customs authorities is recommended as a very effective way for companies to capture and remove counterfeit goods from the market. It also serves to alert Customs officials to the distinguishing differences between genuine and counterfeit products and of the company's specific rights in this regard. They should ensure, too, that business partners, suppliers and staff have all of this information.

In any event, companies should ensure that their brand-enforcement strategy is integrated into their business and branding plans and budget allocations.

For further information (in English) on the activities of the State Administration for Industry and Commerce (SAIC) in developing and enforcing measures to counter intellectual-property infringements, interested readers should visit its website at www.saic.gov.cn

Brand-protection cases in China

In recent years, the sports brand Puma has gained increasing brand awareness and product sales in China and, inevitably, has encountered problems with counterfeiting. In fact, a conservative estimate is that at least 50% of Puma counterfeits come from China—principally sneakers and clothes from Jinjiang and Shishi in Fujian Province, and counterfeit backpacks from Guangzhou in Guangdong Province. Although local law-enforcement agencies have been investigating and punishing counterfeiting practices for more than a dozen years now, their efforts have not proved entirely effective. As for Guangzhou, the counterfeiting of cases and bags is rampant in certain suburbs, where unregistered factories collaborate with foreign trade companies to supply overseas markets.

To counter these activities, Puma's investigators work with the Bureau of Industry and Commerce to track down and prosecute the counterfeiting factories through the court system. (This may entail filing civil suits against websites that sell Puma counterfeits and against exporters of counterfeits.) It has applied for determination and protection as a well-known trademark and works closely with Chinese Customs to enhance IP rights and border protection.

Hiring qualified and experienced private investigators to pursue the counterfeiters is clearly the best course of action for international brands at present, despite the fact that they may feel that this is the responsibility of the local government. In the face of counterfeiting on a massive scale, local government officials are often hampered by a severe shortage of manpower and material resources and by a relative lack of experience of the workings of the market system.

Local fines and forfeitures of counterfeit goods are seldom sufficient in themselves to inflict fatal damage to counterfeiters, who simply resume and redouble their activities to recover their losses. It is therefore incumbent on the international brands to show they are serious about protecting their trademarks by filing claims for damages against the counterfeiters that will make it more difficult for them to pursue their illegal activities. This is more easily said than done, however, because often the primary aim of local law-enforcement officials is to stop specific activities but without destroying the companies involved. This approach may arise from a fear of reprisals or, in some cases, because the officials themselves are implicated in such activities and have a vested interest in seeing them continue.

Measures against the counterfeiters are therefore much more likely to succeed where international brands have sufficient evidence to present to the courts that the damage inflicted by the counterfeiters is on such a scale as to warrant criminal investigation and prosecution. Criminal punishment is the best means of deterrent in China. The jailing of one person will have an explosive effect among other local counterfeiters.

With e-commerce booming, the internet has become the most effective and convenient platform for communication between distributors and manufacturers of counterfeits. International brands need to keep a close eye on large trade websites (such as ebay.com and alibaba.com for international markets, and dangdang.com and taobao.com for domestic Chinese markets) to ensure that these do not become inadvertent tools for the counterfeiters.

As we saw earlier, the PRC's trademark law includes special protection for companies with "well-known trademark" status. Having such a designation can prove very useful to international luxury brands in exerting greater influence on law-enforcement officials, counterfeiters and consumers.

Conclusion

Counterfeiting is a major problem and one that China cannot solve alone. Counterfeiters worldwide are aware of the competitive advantages China has to offer them—low labor and production costs, huge production capacity and high-quality goods—and are keen to make use of these. In that respect, China's counterfeiters are merely responding to international demand.

Experience has shown that the greater the brand awareness an international luxury company commands, the greater is the risk it runs of losing out to counterfeiting activities. While high brand awareness can generate more profits for the brand itself, it can also generate sales of counterfeit goods to those who cannot afford or are unwilling to pay the higher price for the genuine products. Thus, the brands are obliged to spend large sums of money in legal battles to protect their rights against counterfeiters. This is part of the game that a strong luxury brand has to play because, if left unchecked, counterfeits can have a damaging if not fatal impact.

As discussed earlier, the Chinese don't have a strong awareness of intellectual-property rights; indeed, many government officials do not believe that counterfeiting constitutes theft and it is thus way down the list of priorities for public security forces in a country of 1.3 billion people.

At present, local governments that employ anti-counterfeiting officials are financed by local enterprises, which often include counterfeiters themselves. Many of these officials would rather protect their fellow countrymen than the interests of a faceless foreign brand. While the problem of bribery amongst local law-enforcement officials has undoubtedly improved, it still exists and brands should be aware of the measures needed to protect their interests.

ENDNOTES

1 For a breakdown of types of people likely to buy counterfeit products and their motivations for doing so, see Xiao Lu 2008: 130–8.

2 None of his original works remains today. They were collected and buried with Li Shimin, the second emperor of the Tang Dynasty, who adored Wang's works so much that he ordered them to be placed in his grave.

3 Ordish and Adcock 2008: 176.

Liuli Gongfang: Breaking into Luxury by Way of Glass

"Liuli is more than a substance—it is a passion."
Loretta Yang

The company

Liuli Gongfang (琉璃工房, or "LLGF") was set up in 1987 by award-winning Taiwanese actress Loretta Hui-Shang Yang and her film-director husband Yi Chang. Although neither had had any experience of glass blowing, they were willing to risk everything they had to revive a process known as *pâte-de-verre* (lost-wax casting), which mimicked the bronze-making process of the Shang and Zhou dynasties.

Knowing that the glass-blowing methods available to them in Taiwan at that time were not suited to the image they were seeking, the couple devoted themselves to reviving and perfecting a small but important part of China's artistic history. Though the next few years proved to be tough for them financially (to the point where they had to mortgage their homes to keep the business afloat), under the patronage of the Taiwan Ministry of Economics, they were finally able to create an entire collection for an exhibition in Japan in 1991. This was to launch LLGF as a force to be reckoned with on the international stage.

Today, the company has 1,700 employees and 62 boutiques, points of sale and galleries, around the globe. Chang and Yang's glass pieces have also been exhibited at various international galleries and museums, including London's Victoria and Albert, France's Galerie Capazza, and Beijing's Forbidden Palace Museum.

The product

The Chinese characters in the name *liuli* stand for the ancient Chinese word for glass artwork, evoking Chinese traditional culture and spiritual elements in its design concepts. In general today Chinese use the word "*boli*" for the glass they use in daily life. "*Liuli*" sounds more refined and evokes Chinese traditional culture and history.

Hence, Liuli embodies the spirit and verve captured in the company's motto: "To forever create that which is good for the human heart."

Branding is one of Liuli Gongfang's strategies. What is even more crucial is grasping the importance of nurturing a culture and keeping up with the changes of time. Liuli Gongfang is not only about the success of a company, it is about the renaissance of a culture. Through glass, Liuli Gongfang hopes to create a new and modern language that will bring Chinese culture onto the international stage by keeping alive a 3,000-year-old history of glass art. In doing so, it seeks to fuse traditional Chinese ethics and morals with contemporary forms of art, striving to "construct a peaceful society."

LLGF offers a variety of products from collectibles to Liuli Living (glassware, ceramics, tableware, desk accessories, figurines) to jewelry, and each piece tells a story with a uniquely Chinese flavor.

Development in China

Though LLGF began from the island of Taiwan, its business and art has expanded significantly in mainland China. It has opened a workshop in Shanghai and currently has 35 galleries or other points of sale in China's major cities: Beijing, Shanghai, Dalian, Harbin, Chengdu, Guangzhou, Qingdao, Shenzhen, Chongqing, Tianjin, Hangzhou, Xi'an, and Wuhan. In April 2006, it opened its Liuli China Museum near Shanghai's Xintiandi, which features the work of artists from around the world (though, at the time of writing, the museum was relocating).

The company's business achievements have also been impressive. Its annual revenue stands at approximately US$35 million, and its pre-tax profit rate in 2007 was in the region of 10–12%. While Taiwan, Hong Kong and Singapore are major markets for the company, mainland China now accounts for 60% of its revenue, with a profit margin of 20%. Mainland buyers are primarily companies and middle-class Chinese who buy the glassware as sophisticated gifts for friends. Liuli Gongfang will focus on smaller cities such as Suzhou once its position in big cities like Shanghai and Beijing has been firmly established.

Marketing communication

The success of Liuli Gongfang owes a lot to creative marketing strategies which have succeeded in integrating cultural components into the marketing message. Chang and Yang have contributed greatly in promoting awareness of the craft of *liuli*, producing video installations for the China Shanghai International Film Festival in 2007. Their "Presenting Wine" collections were selected to be given as gifts to nominees of the 73rd Oscar awards and the Emmy awards. Most recently, during the 2008 Olympics LLGF's artwork was on display throughout Taiwan's Olympic House of Fortune in Beijing.

The fact that Liuli Gongfang products are on display in prestigious museums around the world differentiates them from ordinary glassware pieces and lifts them into the luxury realm. The company's prestigious artworks include the "Blue Buddha of Medicine" at the Yakushaji temple in Nara, Japan; "A Great Wish," on display in the permanent collection of The National Institute of Women in the Arts in Washington D.C.; "The Great Release of Light," at the

National Palace Museum Collection in Beijing; and "The Proof of
Awareness" at the Corning Museum of Glass.

Yang Hui-Shan and Chang Yi are the living embodiments of
the brand. Their long-standing marriage and their high-profile
collaboration in both the film industry and in Liuli Gongfang
have been widely reported in newspapers and magazines, bringing
valuable publicity to the brand and building emotional ties between
the creators of the glassware and the buyers of the artwork. In the
tradition of Coco Chanel, Louis Vuitton, and Miuccia Prada, the
skills and techniques of the founders are at the company's core and
are being passed on to future generations.

While achieving success in *liuli* production, Yang and Chang
had a wider vision. In 2001, they opened the TMSK Restaurant in
Shanghai's Xin Tian Di district and, later, a TMSK Cafe in central
Beijing. Glassworks are an essential part of the decor in both. Walls,
counters and wine glasses are all made of *liuli* and bathe the restaurants in bright lights and vivid colors. The restaurants serve as a bridge
between LLGF and its potential new glassworks customers, and the
founders have not discounted the possibility of extending this
venture further. In fact, they have established the Shanghai TMSK
Cultural Communications Company to explore new cultural ventures,
such as forming a traditional Chinese music group to play in the restaurants, sponsoring a Chinese classical music competition, and a year-round
Kunqu opera performance in Shanghai. All of these artistic experiments
are an extension of the LLGF glassware business and designed to deliver
their understanding of Chinese culture in a better way.

Major issues

Liuli culture has some limitations in China in that, as we understand it, glass is an art of the Western world. Although the company
is emphasizing its connection with the art in ancient China, the
material and the look of the art pieces is a departure from traditional
Chinese culture. The company's artworks are largely seen as catering to the tastes of the modern world. Finding a workable balance

between the traditional and the modern is a difficult problem which perhaps has yet to be resolved.

Liuli Gongfang's success has given rise to a prosperous market for the glassware industry in China. Thousands of craft workshops have appeared, almost overnight, producing similar-looking products. While none employs the unique manufacturing techniques of Liuli Gongfang, this is not necessarily important to the buyers, and the company has to be careful about the possible damage that these craft workshops can inflict. Many luxury brands have been hurt by counterfeit products, and it remains to be seen whether the company's success can be sustained in the fever of glassware production.

Even if Liuli Gongfang is safe from challenge from the mass-production of glassware because its products are focused on different market segments, then Swarovski and other crystal producers can also present a real problem for the product. Swarovski has a product that is similar in material, and it shines. LLGF also faces competition from the luxury Western tableware competitors such as Daum, Bacarrat and Lalique in China.

LLGF Art Gallery in Shanghai's Plaza 66
Copyright: Elisabeth Peng

China: A Collection of Markets

	GDP per capita RMB (US$)	Rank	GDP (million) RMB (US$)	Rank	Retail sales of consumer goods (million) RMB (US$)	Rank	Population ('000)	Rank
Beijing	49,505 (6,400)	11	772,030 (100,364)	2	327,520 (42,578)	2	15,810	3
Shanghai	57,310 (7,450)	5	1,029,697 (133,861)	1	336,041 (43,685)	1	18,150	2
Tianjin	40,961 (5,325)	14	433,773 (56,390)	6	135,679 (17,638)	6	10,750	5
Chongqing	12,437 (1,616)	41	346,820 (45,086)	7	140,358 (18,246)	5	28,080	1
Province								
Fujian Xiamen	49,887 (6,485)	10	116,237 (15,111)	33	31,494 (4,094)	35	2,330	39
Fuzhou	25,100 (3,263)	29	165,694 (21,540)	28	77,553 (10,082)	24	6,600	21
Futian	15,013 (1,951)	38	42,261 (5,494)	41	14,588 (1,896)	41	2,820	38
Guangdong Shantou	14,943 (1,942)	39	74,092 (9,632)	38	40,060 (5,208)	34	4,953	32
Shenzhen	69,450 (9,028)	2	581,356 (75,576)	4	167,129 (21,727)	4	8,484	10
Guangzhou	63,100 (8,203)	3	606,841 (78,889)	3	218,277 (28,376)	3	9,755	7

Province	City								
	Foshan	50,207 (6,527)	9	292,672 (38,047)	11	77,618 (10,090)	23	5,858	27
	Dongguan	39,931 (5,191)	15	262,463 (34,120)	15	50,000 (6,500)	30	6,748	19
	Zhongshan	33,631 (4,372)	22	81,758 (10,628)	36	27,880 (3,624)	38	2,434	40
	Zuhai	52,317 (6,802)	6	74,980 (9747)	37	25,552 (3,322)	38	1,450	41
Guizhou	Guijang	17,025 (2,217)	37	60,288 (7,837)	40	23,496 (3,054)	39	3,551	35
Hebei	Wuhan	28,461 (3,699)	25	259,000 (33,670)	16	129,333 (16,813)	7	9,100	9
	Tangshan	32,947 (4,283)	23	236,168 (30,702)	20	54,428 (7,076)	28	7,191	16
	Shijazhuang	21,969 (2,856)	32	206,400 (26,832)	23	69,880 (9,084)	25	9,395	8
Henan	Zhengzhou	27,798 (3,613)	27	200,150 (26,019)	24	82,020 (10,663)	20	7,243	15
Heilongjiang	Harbin	21,374 (2,778)	34	209,400 (27,222)	22	69,450 (9,028)	16	9,830	6
Hunan	Changsha	27,853 (3,620)	26	179,066 (23,278)	26	86,561 (11,523)	18	6,465	23
Jilin	Changchun	23,677 (3,078)	31	174,120 (22,636)	27	66,630 (8,662)	27	7,393	14

(Continued)

(Continued)

		GDP per capita RMB (US$)	Rank	GDP (million) RMB (US$)	Rank	Retail sales of consumer goods (million) RMB (US$)	Rank	Population ('000)	Rank
Jiangsu	Wuxi	57,709 (7,502)	4	330,000 (42,900)	9	95,947 (12,473)	14	5,841	28
	Nanjing	39,379 (5,119)	16	277,400 (36,062)	13	116,685 (15,169)	8	7,190	17
	Taizhou	21,491 (2,793)	33	100,250 (13,032)	35	27,133 (3,527)	37	4,634	33
	Suzhou	78,236 (10,171)	1	482,026 (62,663)	5	105,544 (13,721)	11	6,155	24
	Changzhou	37,210 (4,836)	17	156,000 (20,280)	30	51,580 (6,705)	29	3,547	36
	Hulan	13,155 (1,710)	40	65,106 (8,464)	39	23,015 (2,992)	40	5,327	31
Liaoning	Shenyang	35,282 (4,586)	21	248,250 (32,272)	18	104,870 (13,633)	12	7,036	18
	Dalian	42,579 (5,563)	13	256,970 (33,406)	17	83,930 (10,911)	19	5,721	29
Shandong	Qingdao	42,794 (5,562)	12	320,658 (41,685)	10	100,667 (13,087)	13	7,493	13

Province	City							
	Yantai	36,849 (4,790)	20	240,210 (31,227)	19	69,796 (9,073)	26	6,499	22
	Jinan	36,394 (4,731)	19	218,510 (28,406)	21	93,930 (12,211)	15	6,033	26
	Zibo	36,895 (4,796)	18	164,516 (21,387)	29	49,980 (6,497)	31	4,459	34
Shanxi	Taiyuan	29,497 (3,835)	24	101,338 (13,174)	34	43,647 (5,674)	33	3,442	37
Shaanxi	Xi'an	17,794 (2,313)	36	145,002 (18,850)	31	77,620 (10,091)	22	8,230	11
Sichuan	Chengdu	25,950 (3,373)	28	27,500 (3,575)	14	115,530 (15,019)	9	11,034	4
Yunnan	Kunming	19,663 (2,556)	35	120,314 (15,641)	32	48,420 (6,295)	32	6,152	25
Zhejiang	Ningbo	51,285 (6,666)	8	286,450 (37,238)	12	88,250 (11,472)	17	5,604	30
	Hangzhou	51,871 (6,743)	7	344,099 (44,733)	8	111,237 (14,461)	10	6,663	20
	Wenzhou	24,349 (3,165)	30	183,438 (23,847)	25	77,915 (10,129)	21	7,564	12

Source: China Statistical Yearbook, 2007

A Profile of China's Leading Cities

The case of Beijing: Power and wealth

Geography and demographics

Beijing is an ancient city with a long history. Several dynasties (Liao, Jin, Yuan, Ming and Qing) all made Beijing their capital and left the city a legacy of precious cultural treasures: the Great Wall winds for several kilometers in the Beijing area; the Summer Palace is a classic composition of ancient royal gardens, and the Forbidden City is one of the largest royal palaces in the world; and Tiantan is where the emperors used to fete their ancestors. While these four sites have been accorded world cultural heritage status by UNESCO, perhaps the best representatives of Beijing are the vanishing *hutongs* and square courtyards. Through hundreds of years, they have become the symbol of Beijing life. In preparation for the 2008 Olympic Games, the city's entire infrastructure was updated and a series of post-modern buildings (National Stadium, National Opera, CCTV, China World Tour 3, and so on) have changed the face of Beijing so that it now combines tradition and modernity.

Beijing is the political center of the whole "middle kingdom." All the central government organizations, ministries, military and media groups are concentrated around the Forbidden City. Because of downtown space limitations, the CBD developed in the eastern suburbs of Beijing and this has become home to most of the landmark luxury businesses in places such as the Yintai Center and Shin Kong Place.

In terms of economic development, Beijing is the second-largest city in China, behind only Shanghai in economic and industrial production. The service and finance sectors contribute 76% to Beijing's GDP. The financial sector controls more than 90% of the nation's credit capital and 65% of its insurance capital. According to *Fortune* magazine, of the 500 biggest multinational companies, 293 have their Greater China or Asia-Pacific headquarters in Beijing.

Beijing also has the most important resources for education and research. More than 15% of Chinese universities and 60% of national research centers are located here and many multinational companies also have research centers here. The city is also the art, media and sports center of China, and is home to a great many artists and celebrities—painters, movie stars, musicians, Olympic medalists, directors, producers and so on, creating a very rich and vivid cultural environment.

According to the Beijing Municipal Bureau of Statistics, at the end of 2008, China's capital had a population of 16.95 million, up 620,000 from a year earlier. Beijing's cultural, political and economic concentration provides a huge base of potential consumers of luxury goods. As discussed earlier, Beijingers are more culturally oriented than their counterparts in other parts of China. They buy luxury brands because they appreciate their values and designs, not simply for the flashy logo.

Because of the city's special profile, the main luxury consumers include high-level government officials, CEOs of state-owned banks and companies, successful businessmen, movie and sports stars, high-tech yuppies, and tourists. Luxury consumers also include institutions, such as lobbyists and government organizations.

FIGURE B1: *Map of Beijing*

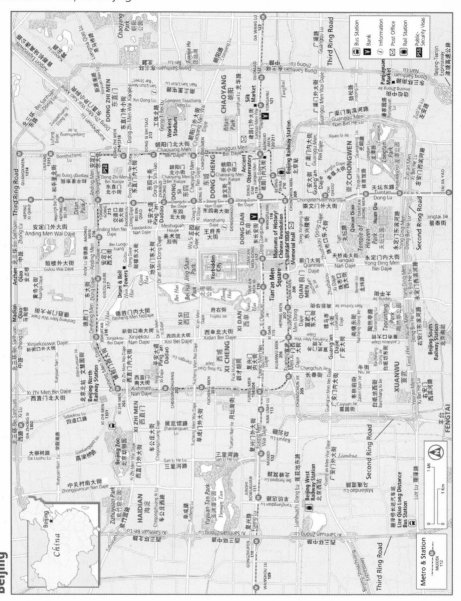

Source: Jen Lin-Liu and Sherisse Pham, *Frommer's Beijing*, 5th Edition, Frommers, 2008

Macroeconomic review

In 2008, Beijing's nominal GDP was the equivalent of about US$147 billion, a year-on-year growth of 13.4%. Its GDP per capita was US$8,000. Beijing's tertiary industries represent 73% of the total GDP. Urban disposable income per capita was US$3,636, a real increase of 7% over the previous year.

Beijing's real estate and automobile sectors have continued to blossom in recent years. In 2007, a total of 23 million square meters of housing real estate was sold. At the end of 2008, Beijing had 3.18 million automobiles registered, a year-on-year increase of 14.5%.

Boosted by the Olympics, in 2008 Beijing achieved retail sales growth of 21.6% and, for the first time ever, overtook Shanghai to become China's leading city in retail sales.

TABLE B1: *Beijing's economic performance 2001–2008*

	2001	2002	2003	2004	2005	2006	2007	2008
GDP Growth	11.0%	10.2%	10.5%	13.2%	11.1%	12%	13%	13.4%
China GDP	7.3%	8.9%	9.1%	9.5%	9.9%	11.1%	11.4%	9%
Retail Sales Growth	10.4%	9.5%	14.5%	15.3%	10.8%	13%	16.8%	21.6%

Source: Beijing Bureau of Statistics

The main commercial areas

As a political and cultural center, commerce seems to take second place in the municipality's priority list. However, because of the purchasing power of the local consumers, Beijing has five very active main commercial areas: Wangfujing, Guomao, Xidan, Qianmen and Zhongguancun. Historically, Beijing's commercial areas were located in the east and south of the city, and little has changed today, especially for luxury shopping. The main exceptions to this are Xidan, situated in the west, and Zhongguancun, a new commercial area in the north where high-technology companies and the main universities and research centers are located.

The luxury shopping blocks

The CBD

The Beijing CBD, running from Guomao to Shing Kong Place, occupies almost four square kilometers of the Chaoyang District on the east side of the city and is the primary area of finance, media, and business services. It is home to a variety of corporate regional headquarters (such as the new Chinese Central Television Center (CCTV), and the new Beijing television center (BTV)), shopping malls, and high-end residences. It has attracted 117 Fortune 500 businesses in the financial, media, information technology, consulting and service industries. More than 60% of overseas-funded companies in Beijing are located in the CBD. A majority of foreign embassies are now concentrated in and around the CBD. The area houses six luxury shopping centers: China World Mall, Yintai Center, Shin Kong Place, Scitech Center, The Lufthansa Center (Yan Sha) and Sanlitun Village.

The China World Trade Center, a landmark for luxury business since the early 1990s, is a hybrid area incorporating high-end offices, three five-star hotels, serviced luxury apartments and a luxury shopping mall housing top brand names such as Louis

Dolce & Gabbana and Cartier flagship stores in Beijing's Yintai Center
Copyright: Pierre Xiao Lu

Vuitton, Hermes, Gucci, Dior, dunhill, Prada, Salvatore Ferragamo, Cartier, Van Cleef & Arpels, and many more.

Nearby, the INTIME (Yintai) Center is a huge high-end residential and business area linked with Jianwai Soho. Hotel Park Hyatt opened in the Center and many luxury brands—including Giorgio Armani, Dolce & Gabbana, Ermenegildo Zegna, Cartier, Tourbillon, Hermès and Shanghai Tang—have opened flagship stores there.

Shin Kong Place is located to the east of the CBD, next to Soho city and Hua Mao, two high-end residential areas for the newly wealthy, and close to Wanda Plaza, a hybrid shopping center, the Sofitel and Ritz-Carlton Hotels and many high-end clubs and restaurants. This department store is a joint venture between Taiwanese Shin Kong MIT Sukoshi, and Hualian, one of the biggest Chinese retailing groups. Because of its location and excellent shopping environment, this new store has become the new luxury shopping landmark in Beijing, featuring brands such as Chanel, Gucci, Zegna, Burberry, Bottega Veneta, Chaumet, Bvlgari, Prada, Salvatore Ferragamo, and many more. Fauchon opened its first Boulangerie-Café in China there.

The Scitech Center (Sai Te), located on the west side of the CBD in the old embassy district, is a traditional high-end shopping center, housing Piaget's flagship store and a Bentley dealership on the ground floor. However, after experiencing some management problems, the shopping center was taken over and restructured by Ports International in 2008. It is still very influential in high-end product sales because of some loyal wealthy clients from the northeast provinces (Heilongjiang, Jilin, Liaoning) and Shanxi Province.

The Lufthansa Center (Yan Sha), located on the north side of the CBD, is a hybrid area housing a number of embassies, high-end office buildings, five-star hotels, serviced luxury apartments and international schools. Although now becoming somewhat dated, it still has lots of loyal shoppers, particularly among the expat community living around the center. In 2008, Solana, a new middle-range shopping mall located next to the Lufthansa Center, opened and will attract more consumers to this area.

Located in the diplomatic area famous for its pubs and bars, Sanlitun Village—a community of 19 dramatic buildings—was inspired by Japanese architect Kengo Kuma and developed by Hong Kong's Swire Group. High-end lifestyle brands such as BMW Lifestyle, Adidas, Puma, Apple, Lacoste, Chow Tai Fook Fine Jewellery and Chow Sang Sang have located their biggest stores here.

Sanlitun Village, with fashion and high-end lifestyle brands
Copyright: Pierre Xiao Lu

The Wangfujing Area

In the Wangfujing area there are three important luxury shopping malls: the Peninsula Hotel, Oriental Plaza and Jin Bao Place. The Peninsula Palace Hotel (Wang Fu Hotel) was one of the first five-star luxury hotels in mainland China. Its strategic location, near the Forbidden City and Tiananmen Square and in the middle of the Wangfujing traditional commercial area, meant that it quickly became a landmark for many luxury companies seeking to develop a market in China market. Almost every successful luxury brand in China started by opening a store in the shopping mall of the Peninsula Hotel. Hermès, Louis Vuitton, Chanel, Zegna and Prada are among the many to do so. Despite the fact that the biggest store in the mall cannot exceed 300 square meters, it is the dream of every luxury brand to have a *pied à terre* there, even today when there are so many alternative venues.

Like the Peninsula Hotel, Oriental Plaza (Dong Fang Square) is located in the Wangfujing area, but on the north side of Chang'an Avenue next to the Beijing Hotel and opposite the Ministry of Commerce. It is a hybrid business area, with a huge volume of tourists and business people. Built by Hong Kong tycoon Li Ka Shing, this project has established itself as the most visited shopping mall in Beijing, with millions of domestic and international tourists every year. The ground floor of the plaza is occupied by brands like Zegna, Valentino, Burberry, MaxMara, Bally, Dunhill, Tiffany, Kenzo, Jaeger-LeCoultre, S.T. Dupont, and Rolex.

Jin Bao Street, owned and developed by Hong Kong's Fu Wah International Group, houses top-notch hotels such as the Regent Beijing, Park Plaza Beijing, Legendale Palace Hotel and Xinhai Jinjiang, and high-end offices including Jin Bao Tower and Huali Tower. Key government bodies such as Dongcheng District Executive

New Jinbao Street project with gigantic Gucci store occupying ground and first floors prior to opening in early 2009
Copyright: Pierre Xiao Lu

Service Center as well as Hong Kong Jockey Club Beijing Clubhouse are all a stone's throw away. High-end serviced apartments and commercial properties were completed at the end of 2008. Jin Bao Street has already attracted famous brands and companies, including Rolls Royce, Ferrari, Lamborghini, Maserati, Ogilvy, JWT and the Li & Fung Group. Gucci, Burberry and Bottega Veneta have opened stores in Jin Bao Place. The famous Da Dong, a high-end Beijing duck restaurant, is located on the top floor of the mall.

Beijing Financial Street and Xidan area

Beijing Financial Street—the country's most important financial center—is located inside the 2nd Ring Road, on the west side of Beijing city, next to the traditional commercial area—Xidan. Its 35 blocks are home to foreign and domestic financial institutions and Chinese regulatory agencies such as the People's Bank of China (PBOC), China Banking Regulatory Commission (CBRC), China Securities Regulatory Commission (CSRC), and China Insurance Regulatory Commission (CIRC). With assets totaling RMB3 trillion (US$1.9 trillion) and a daily cash flow exceeding RMB10 billion (US$1.5 billion), Beijing Financial Street accounts for 60% of the country's financial assets. It controls 90% of national loans and 65% of national insurance premiums, which makes Beijing the country's largest monetary and financial market. Seasons Place is

Seasons Place in Beijing Financial Street seen from Westin Hotel, 2009
Copyright: Pierre Xiao Lu

the only shopping mall in the area, and the Ritz-Carlton, Westin, Intercontinental and Marriott hotels all chose this area to open their first five-star hotels in Beijing. Louis Vuitton opened its third Beijing store in the mall. Dior, Dior Homme, Gucci, Versace, Zegna, Hugo Boss, Berluti, St.John, Cerruti 1881, a.testoni, Girard-Perregaux, Jaeger-LeCoultre, Omega, Chopard, and IWC all have stores on the ground floor.

Xidan is the traditional shopping area for young people. The new Joy City shopping center (developed by China's powerful Cofco Group) provides a very comfortable shopping environment offering world-famous brand names or mid-range and high-end local brand names. Above the seven floors of retail space, the center also provides apartment and hotel accommodation.

Joy City attracts fashionable young people to the Xidan area
Copyright: Pierre Xiao Lu

Qianmen area

The Qianmen area, located on the south side of Tiananmen Square, is one of the most prestigious of the city's traditional shopping areas, where famous Chinese brands such as Tong Shenghe, Bu Liansheng, Qian Xiangyi, and Quan Jude first established their business. The area has been undergoing progressive renovation, the first phase of which was completed in early 2009. In 2008, Patek Philippe opened its second Chinese store here (the first being on the Bund in Shanghai).

Renovated Dashilan Street in the Qianmen area has a huge volume of consumers attracted by the traditional Chinese architecture even though the majority of the stores are yet to be occupied
Copyright: Pierre Xiao Lu

The specific case of Shanghai

Geography

With a population of some 18.45 million at the end of 2008, Shanghai is China's most populous city and one of the largest metropolitan areas in the world, with a total land area of more than 6,000 sq km. Located at the mouth of the Yangtze River on China's central eastern coast, the city is administered as a municipality.

FIGURE B2: *Map of Shanghai*

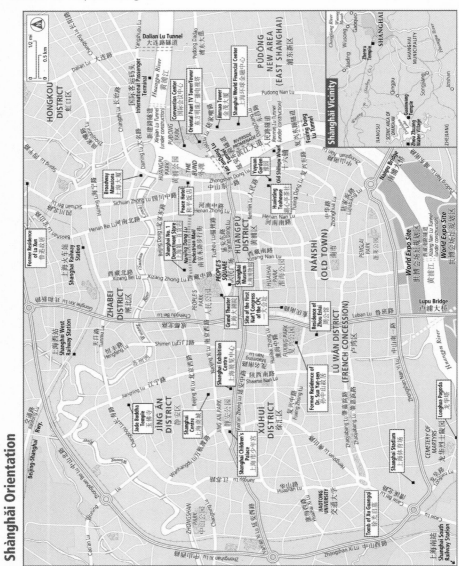

Source: Sharon Owyang, *Frommer's Shanghai, 5th Edition, Frommers, 2008*

Shanghai, which means "on the sea," was originally a fishing and textiles town. It grew to importance in the nineteenth century because of its favorable port location and was one of the cities opened to foreign trade by the 1842 Treaty of Nanking after the first Opium War. The city flourished as a center of commerce between east and west, and became a multinational hub of finance and business by the 1930s. The economic reforms introduced since 1979 have resulted in further development such that in 2005 Shanghai became the world's busiest cargo port. The city is an emerging tourist destination, renowned for its historical landmarks such as the Bund and Xintiandi, its modern and ever-expanding Pudong skyline (including the Oriental Pearl Tower), and its new reputation as a cosmopolitan center of culture and design. Today, Shanghai is the largest center of commerce and finance in mainland China, and has been described as the "showpiece" of the world's fastest-growing economy. The whole city is still undergoing massive renovation projects in preparation for WorldExpo in 2010.

Macroeconomic review

Shanghai's economic growth progressed at a rapid pace, with a double-digit increase for each of the 16 years to 2007. The financial crisis of 2008 meant that growth slowed somewhat but still achieved a very respectable 9.7%.

TABLE B2: *Shanghai's economic indicators*

Indicators	2001	2002	2003	2004	2005	2006	2007	2008
GDP Growth	10.20%	10.90%	11.80%	13.60%	11.10%	12%	13.3%	9.7%
China GDP	7.3%	8.9%	9.1%	9.5%	9.9%	11.1%	11.4%	9%
Retail Sales Growth	8.1%	9.3%	9.1%	10.5%	11.5%	13%	14.5%	17.9%
China Price Index Growth	0.70%	−0.80%	1.20%	2.20%	1.00%	1.2%	3.2%	5.8%
Avg. Disposal Income Growth	9.94%	2.85%	12.20%	12.21%	10.9%	11.8%	14.3%	13%

Source: Shanghai Statistics Bureau

The commercial areas

Though Shanghai has many more commercial areas than Beijing, its shopping malls are normally middle-range and for ordinary citizens and tourists, and there are fewer high-end and luxury shopping centers.

The main commercial areas are Nanjing Road, Huaihai Road, People's Square, Xujiahui, Hongqiao and Lujiazui area in Pudong. The city hall and major administration units are located in People's Square in Huangpu District, which also serve as a commercial area, including the famous Nanjing Road. Other major commercial areas include the classy Xintiandi and Huaihai Road in Luwan district and Xujiahui in Xuhui District. Lujiazui is the commercial center of Pudong area.

Nanjing Road, divided into two distinct areas by People's Square, is China's premier shopping street. To the east, from the Bund to the Square, it caters mainly to domestic tourists and is often packed with people on weekends and holidays. The west side, which runs from the Square to Jing'an Temple, is the most chic street in Shanghai and home to important luxury shopping centers such as Plaza 66, City Place, Meilongzhen Isetan, JiuGuang and Shanghai City.

Local people, who often look down on Nanjing East Road and its domestic shoppers from other provinces, generally cannot afford the luxury goods in Nanjing West Road, and therefore shop at fashionable but middle-range Huaihai Road (another busy shopping boulevard with more-affordable upscale stores) instead.

The luxury shopping blocks

There are four luxury shopping blocks situated in the different divisions of Shanghai: The Bund area, West Nanjing Road, Xintiandi and the Pudong area. The large shopping malls (Plaza 66, City Plaza, Meilongzhen Plaza, and Jiuguang Mall) situated at the western end of Nanjing West Road, near the Jing'an Temple, host the most famous names.

Three on the Bund (featuring Giorgio Armani's flagship store in China) and the Bund 18 complement the area's status as Shanghai's

Fifth Avenue. The Bund area is undergoing a total renovation in preparation for WorldExpo in 2010 and important high-end retailers such as New York's Saks Fifth Avenue and the Swatch Group plan to open department stores and flagship stores in the area.

Middle Huaihai Road and Xintiandi offer international-style department stores in the former French Concession area. Dunhill and Vacheron Constantin from Richemont have their flagship stores here and Hermès is planning a private club boutique in the area.

SHANGHAI'S TOP FOUR LUXURY SHOPPING MALLS

Plaza 66

Address: 1266 Nanjing West Road

Brands: Dior, Chanel, Fendi, Hermès, Louis Vuitton, Lanvin, Gucci, Emporio Armani, Armani Jeans, Versace, Celine, Cartier, Loewe, Ermenegildo Zegna, Hugo Boss, A/T Atsuro Tayama, Escada, Prada, Just Cavali, Lancel, Tod's, Dior Homme, G. F. Ferre, Bulgari, Mikimoto, Piaget, Pal Zileri, St.John, dunhill, Laurel, D&G, Escada Sports, Diesel, BCBG, TSE, Anteprima, Panerai, Ascot Chang, Pal Zileri/Pull.

City Plaza

Address: 1618 Nanjing West Road

Brands: Givenchy, Lagerfeld, Kenzo, MaxMara, Chloé, Swarovski, Bally, Guy Laroche, Armani Colezioni, A|X Armani Exchange, Trussardi, Mont Blanc, Y-3, Evisu, Lottusse, Max & Co.

This new mega-mall features an eight-floor department store, a sparkling supermarket in the basement and a new Jean-Paul Gaultier store on the ground floor.

Three on the Bund

Address: 3 Zhong Shan Dong Yi Road

Brands: Giorgio Armani, Emporio Armani, Armani Jeans, YSL Rive Gauche, John Galliano, Marni, Yohji Yamamoto, Vivian Tam, CP Company, Stone Island, Y's, Ann Demeulemeester, Bottega Veneta, Costume National

Three on the Bund brings together all aspects of contemporary living: art, culture, food, fashion and music. Giorgio Armani opened its 1,100-square-metre flagship store in the landmark seven-storey historical building.

18 on the Bund

Address: 18 Zhong Shang Dong Yi Road

Brands: Cartier, Zegna, Patek Philippe, Boucheron, Ports 1961, Ulysse Nardin

The building formerly known as the Macquarie Bank Tower was the headquarters of the Chartered Bank of Australia, India and China and was built in 1923. Totally renovated, it was reopened in 2004 and received some of the world's top luxury brands on the ground and first floors. It also houses leading French, Italian and Chinese restaurants, and lounge bars offering beautiful views of the Huangpu River and the new Pudong area.

The Lujiazui area in Pudong is another very important commercial district for luxury and high-end brands, being home to Super Brand Mall (Zhengda Square) and Yaohan (Babaiban) Shopping Mall. Two new luxury landmarks are also currently under construction: Shanghai World Financial Center and International Financial Center.

Another interesting area is the Hongqiao area, which is home to large numbers of foreign residents, notably from Japan, Korea,

Hong Kong and Taiwain. Their strong buying power means that even the retail prices in the local Carrefour store are higher than those in other parts of Shanghai. The LVMH group is building its own department store there and plans to open in 2010.

In Beijing, it is Joy City which attracts fashionable young people; in Shanghai, Raffles City in People's Square plays a similar role. This project is developed and managed by Singapore's CapitaLand.

Rental prices

International luxury brands are optimistic about the potential growth of the domestic market, increasing the demand for retail property in Shanghai. High demand and a shortage of retail property have caused the retail rental market to rise. At the end of 2008, a first-floor retail fashion space of less than 200sqm in shopping centers in central Shanghai commanded an average rent of US$105/sqm/month, and further increases were expected in 2009.

Retail space in the Nanjing East Road region is the most expensive, with an average rent of US$142/sqm/month. The area's high

FIGURE B3: *Retail rental trends, 2000–2007*

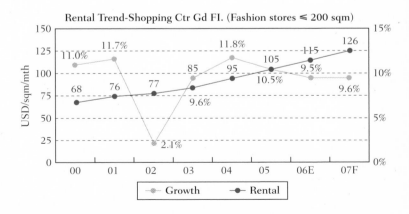

Source: Colliers International Property Report, 2007.

density of retail shops popular with large numbers of local interstate tourists pushs rents higher. Nanjing West Road attracts a high density of international luxury brands and, as a consequence, retail rents are also high, averaging US$138/sqm/month. Overall, the rentals in the Xujiahui area have witnessed the fastest growth, increasing at 17% annually in the four years to 2007.

FIGURE B4: *Average rentals of Shanghai's shopping centers, by district*

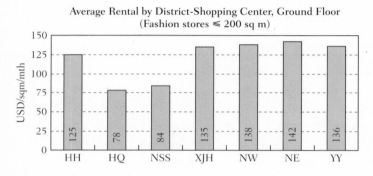

Source: Colliers International Shanghai
Key: HH: Huaiha Rd; HQ: Hongqiao; NSS: New Shanghai Store; XJH: Xujiahui; NW: Nanjing West Rd; NE: Nanjing East Rd; YY: Yu Yuan.

China's Magazine Market

	Field	Arrival in China	Publisher	Chinese Partner	Coverage	Circulation	Distribution	Readership
Vogue	Fashion for Women	2005	Condé Nast Asia-Pacific	China Pictorial	First-/Second-Tier Cities	400,000	Subscription 15% Retailing 15% Remaining details unavailable	Age group: Mainly 25–40 years old Monthly income: Higher than average Education: Mostly university graduates or above Occupation: White-collar worker 48.1%; Private business 10.4%; Student 14.3%; Other 27.2%
Elle	Fashion for Women	1987	Hachette Filipacchi	Shanghai Translation Publishing House	First-/Second-Tier Cities	505,320	Newsstand 67% Supermarket 10% Airport & Intl Flight 4.5% Subscription 8% Bookstore 3.5% Subway newsstand 7%	Age group: 20–24 48% 25–29 28% 30–34 12% Other 12% Monthly income (RMB): Average individual 2,629 (approx. US$400*) Education: University or above 79% Occupation: Middle/Senior level manager 26%; Office worker 40%; Entrepreneur 5%

Magazine	Focus	Year	Category	Regulator	Cities	Circulation	Distribution	Demographics
Cosmopolitan	Fashion for Women	1993	Trends Magazines	National Tourism Administration	First-/Second-Tier Cities	658,000	Subscription 4.3% Subway 11% Airport 6% Supermarket 4% Other 7%	Age group: 18–24 15.6% 25–29 36.7% 35–39 26.8% 35–45 20.9% Monthly income (RMB): Average individual 8,195 (US$1,200) Education: Senior middle school 1.8%; College 23.1%; University 68.9%; Higher 6.2%
Harper's Bazaar	Fashion for Women	2001	Trends Magazines	National Tourism Administration	First-/Second-Tier Cities	262,000	Newsstand 54% Supermarket 18% Subscription 13% Bookstore 7% Airport & Intl Flight 4% Overseas 2% Hotel 1%	Age group: 18–24 21% 25–29 36% 30–34 23% 35–45 21% Monthly income (RMB): Average individual 5,914 (US$900) 4,000–6,999 (US$600–1,000) 92%; 7,000–9,999 (US$1,000–1500) 6%; above 10,000 (US$1,500) 2% Occupation: Company managerial staff 32%

(Continued)

	Field	Arrival in China	Publisher	Chinese Partner	Coverage	Circulation	Distribution	Readership
								Company staff 30%; Specialist 19%; Owner of private firm 8%; Entertainer 2%; Other 9%
Marie Claire	Fashion for Women	2002	Hachette Filipacchi	China Sports Publications Corporation	First-/Second-Tier Cities	167,000	Newsstand 74% Supermarket 10% Subway 6% Subscription 5% Airport 3% Bookstore 2%	Age group: 20–24 55% 25–29 24% 30–35 15% >35 6% Education: Bachelor's degree or above 90% Occupation: Mid/senior-level management 26%; White-collar worker 32%; Entrepreneur 5% Monthly income (RMB): Average individual 2,467 (US$362) Average household 5, 512 (US$810)
Ray Li *Accessories and Beauty*	Fashion, Cosmetics, Lifestyle for Women	2000	Boda (44% Gruner + Jahr, Bertelsmann)	China Light Industry Press	First-/Second-Tier Cities	1,649,000	Newsstand/kiosk 70% Subway 10% Chain store 9% Subscription 4% Bookstore 1%	Age group: <18 4% 18–24 38% 25–29 26% >30 32%

Magazine	Content	Year	Publisher	Cities	Circulation	Distribution	Demographics
						Hotel, restaurant, office building 1% Other 5%	Education: Below junior college 2%; Junior college 25%; Bachelor's degree 46%; Postgraduate degree 27% Occupation: High-level white-collar worker 49%; Company employee 12%; Government employee 12%; Freelancer 12%; Private business person 15% Monthly income (RMB): <3,000 (US$441) 7%; 3,000–5,000 (US$441–735) 28%; 5,001–8,000 (US$735–1,176) 44%; >8,000 (US$1,176) 21%
Ray woman & vogue	Fashion, Cosmetics, Lifestyle for Women	2000	Boda (44% Gruner + Jahr, Bertelsmann)	China Light Industry Press	First-/Second-Tier Cities	900,000	Newsstand/kiosk 68% Subway 10% Supermarket 9% Subscription 4% Hotel, restaurant, office building 2% Bookstore 2% Other 5%	Age group: <23 8% 23–27 25% 28–31 29% >32 38% Education: Junior college and below 43%; Bachelor's degree 43%; Postgraduate 14% Occupation: High-level white collar worker 34%; Company employee 24%; Government employee 11%

(Continued)

Field	Arrival in China	Publisher	Chinese Partner	Coverage	Circulation	Distribution	Readership
							Freelancer 6%; Private business person 3%; Monthly income (RMB): <2,000 (US$294) 12%; 2,000–5,000 (US$294–735) 51%; 5,001–8,000 (US$ 735–1,176) 28%; >8001 (US$1,176) 9%
FHM Men's Monthly Magazine		Trends Magazines	National Tourism Administration	First-/Second-Tier Cities	512,000	Newsstand 67% Subscription 12% Subway 3.5% Airport & Int flight 8% Hotel 6% Supermarket 2.5% Other 1%	Age group: <24 17.1% 25–34 53.4% 35–44 22.0% >45 7.5% Education: High school 9.7% College 77.3% Master's degree or above 13% Annual income (RMB): <50,000 (US$7,352) 19.3%; 50,000–100,000 (US$7,352–14,705) 24.6%; 100,000–200,000 (US$ 14705–29411) 33.2%; >200,000(US$29,411) 22.9%
Vogue Men Men's Fashion (April and Sept.)		Condé Nast Asia-Pacific	China Pictorial	First-/Second-Tier Cities,	400,000	N/A	Targets successful men aged 28–40

Title	Type	Publisher	Group	Distribution area	Circulation	Channels	Reader profile
Bazaar Men	Men's Fashion Bi-Monthly	Trends Magazines	National Tourism Administration	First-/Second-Tier Cities	370,000	Newsstand 54% Subscription 18% Supermarket 16% Bookstore 9% Hotel 3%	Average age 31.5 years old, with average annual income RMB165,802 (US$24,383) Stylish, well-educated and in senior positions across range of occupations
Trends Esquire	Men's Fashion Monthly	Trends Magazines	National Tourism Administration	First-/Second-Tier Cities	538,730	Newsstand 57.7% Airport 1% Subway 4.5% Subscription 15% Bookstore 4.3% Supermarket 17% Internet 0.5%	Age group: 18–29 45.30% 30–34 31.90% 35–39 16.90% 40–45 5.80% Education: College: 17.4%; University 65.1%; Postgraduate 17.5% Annual income — family (RMB): <40,000 (US$5,882) 8.4%; 40,000–80,000 (US$5,882—11,765) 28.4%; 80,000–120,000 (US$11,765–17,647) 37.5%; 120,000–300,000 (US$17,647–44,118) 23.3%; >300,000 (>US$44,118) 6.1%
L'officiel Hommes	Men's Fashion Bi-Monthly	Fashion Magazine	Chinese Federation of Literature and Art Circles	First-/Second-Tier Cities	350,000	N/A	New metropolitan young men; mainly 25–35 years old; average monthly income RMB6,000 +; pursue fashion, high-end

(Continued)

Field	Arrival in China	Publisher	Chinese Partner	Coverage	Circulation	Distribution	Readership
							technologies; most of them are well-educated; their occupations are IT, creative, telecom, etc...
Men's Uno — Men's Fashion Monthly		Men's Uno Magazine	China National Silk Import and Export Corporation	First-/Second-Tier Cities	328,000	Newsstand 69% Post office 8% Supermarket 10% Bookstore 7% Airport and hotel lobby 6%	Age group: <24 15% 25–30 41% 31–36 32% >37 12% Income (RMB): <4,000 (US$588) 10%; 4,000–6,999 (US$588–1,029) 25%; 7,000–9,999 (US$1,029–1,470) 40%; >10,000 (US$1,470) 25%
Men's Health — Men's Health Monthly		Trends Magazines	National Tourism Administration	First-/Second-Tier Cities	413,700	Newsstand 67% Airport 9% Hotel 6% Subway 3.5% Subscription 12% Supermarket 2.5%	Age group: 19–24 9% 25–34 63% 35–40 22% 40–45 6% Education: Junior college 6%; College & university 75.4%; Postgraduate and above 18.6% Occupation: IT & telecommunications 25%; Joint-venture corporation 42%; Financial 10%; Medicine & law 15%; Professional 5%

Fortune	Business	1999	Time Inc.	CCI Asia-Pacific Limited	First-/Second-/Third-Tier Cities	181,280	Non-paid Subscription	Other 3% Annual income (RMB): <40,000 (US$5,882) 4.2%; 40,000–60,000 (US$5,882–8,823) 12.1%; 60,000–80,000 (US$8,823–11,765) 25.1%; 80,000–100,000 (US$11,765–14,706) 18.1%; >100,000 (<US$14,706) 36.5% <u>Age group:</u> <25 1% 26–35 38% 36–55 52% <55 9% male 84% female 15% Education: Master's or Doctorate 32% College or University 66% Other 2% <u>Occupation:</u> CEO/president/owner/partner/ director/vice-/manager/CFO/ CMO/COO 79.5% Professional 5.8% Government officer and other 14.7% <u>Type of Business:</u> State-owned enterprise 14.5% Foreign enterprise 24.4% Private enterprise 26.6% Government 3.3% Joint-stock company 19.5% Other 11.7%

(Continued)

	Field	Arrival in China	Publisher	Chinese Partner	Coverage	Circulation	Distribution	Readership
Forbes	Business	2003	Forbes Inc.	Direct Marketing of Asia Limited	First-/Second-Tier Cities	138,000	Free distribution at airports, five-star hotels, clubs, EMBA schools and high-end consumer outlets	Occupation: Senior-level executive 90.4%; (Chairman/President/Director/ VP/Owner/Partner/CEO/COO/ CFO/CIO/Chief Engineer/ General Manager/Factory Director/Sales/Marketing Director) Officer/Professional 1.4% Average annual income (RMB): Individual 177,000; Family 284,000
Harvard Business Review China	Business Management	2002	Business Review	China Institute of Social Science	First-/Second-Tier Cities	125,000	Paid subscription 87% Controlled copy 10% Retail 3%	Occupation: Director/partner/president/ GM/VP/Professinass 56%; Department/project manager 39%; Other 5% Annual family income (RMB): 1,000,000 (US$147,059) or above 6%; 300,000–1,000,000 (US$44,148–147,059) 34%; 200,000–300,000 (US$29,412–44,148) 27%; 200,000 or below 33%; Readers' company size (person): 1,000 or above 28.4%

Name	Type	Year	Publisher (International)	Publisher (China)	Distribution	Circulation	Distribution Channels	Readership
								500–1,000 8.4% 100–500 38.7% 100 or below 24.5% Readers'z companies sales revenue (RMB): 1 billion or more 28.1%; 100 million–1 billion 34.7%; 50 million–100 million 8.5%; 50 million or less 27.7% Type of Business: Manufacturing 25%; IT/Telecom 16%; Wholesale/Retail/Trade 10%; Finance/Insurance/Banking 8%; Consultant/Market Research 8%; Healthcare 6% Real Estate 5%; Logistics 4% Ad/PR/Media 4%; Other 15%
BusinessWeek	Business	1986	McGraw-Hill Companies, Inc. of the United States	China Commerce and Trade Press (China's Ministry of Commerce)	First-/Second-/Third-Tier Cities	160,000	Retailing (single copy sales) 28.8% Paid subscription 10.6% Non-paid subscription 60.6%	Age group: 15–24 3.4% 25–34 38.8% 35–44 31.9% 45–54 19.5% 55+ 6.4% Male 67% Female 33% Education: Postgraduate or above 8.3%; College or University 80.5%; Other 11.2% Occupation: Board Members 32.8%;

(Continued)

Field	Arrival in China	Publisher	Chinese Partner	Coverage	Circulation	Distribution	Readership
							GM/CEO/President 31.4%; Legal Representatives 15.2%; Academic 5%; Director/Manager 30%; Professional 19%; CFO/CIO/CMO/Other Chief Officers 6%; Government Officials 8% Annual income (RMB): <60,000 (US$8,823) 22.1%; 60,000–120,000 (US$8,823–17,647) 31.4%; 120,000–300,000 (US$17,647–44,118) 32.7%; 300,000–500,000 (US$44,118–73,529) 10.9%
China Entrepreneur	1985	The Economic Daily		First-/Second-Tier Cities	172,687	Paid subscription (post office, direct retailing) 46% Retailing (airport, hotel, supermarket, bookstore, newsstand) 28% Non-paid subscription 26%	Age group: <30 18% 30–39 40% 40–49 32% >50 10% male 85% female 15% Education: Master's/Doctorate 14%; College/ University 78%; Junior college and below 8% Occupation: President/GM 29%; Vice-/CEO 27%;

| 21st Century Business Herald | Business | 2004 | Nanfang Media Group | First-/Second-/Third-Tier Cities | 150,084 | Paid subscription 35% Non-paid subscription 65% Post office 25% Retailing (bookstore, retailing) 10% Public 65% | Government officer 6%; Manager/Director 20%; Professional 8%; Type of Business: Foreign capital/joint venture corporation 22%; Government 10%; State-owned enterprise 30%; Private enterprise 36%; Other 2% Annual income (RMB): <100,000 (US$14,706) 10%; 100,000–300,000 (US$14,706–44,118) 33%; 300,000–1,000,000 (US$44,118–147,059) 15%; 1,000,000–2,000,000 (US$147,059–294,118) 28%; >2,000,000 (US$294,118) 14% |
| 21st Century Business Review | | | | | | | Age group: 35–44 46% 45–59 42% Male 74% Female 26% Education: Postgraduate and above 46%; College & University 40%; Senior high school and below 14% Occupation: Middle manager 11%; Senior manager 53%; |

(Continued)

	Field	Arrival in China	Publisher	Chinese Partner	Coverage	Circulation	Distribution	Readership
								Other 36% Monthly income (RMB): 7,001–9,000 (US$1,030–1,323) 6%; >18,000 (US$2,647) 94%
Tatler	Lifestyle	2002	Edipresse Group	Edipresse Asia	First-Tier Cities	60,000	Subscription 8% VIP 42.1% Newsstand 19.2% Hotel 12.7% Airport 1.7% Private chamber/Golf Club 3.5% Financial institution 3.6% Other 9.2%	Male 45% Female 55% Average age 34.35 Education: Postgraduate or above 6%; College or University 88%; Other 6% Marital status: Married 59%; Single 40% Other 1%; Occupation: CEO/President 29%; GM/Vice-President 21%; CFO/Director 14%; Owner/Partner 18%; Manager 7%; Department Director 4%; Professional 6%; Other 1%
Noblesse	Lifestyle	2004	Noblesse	Anhui Art Publishing House	First-/Second-Tier Cities	103,000	Member delivery 13% Non-paid subscription 40% Retail display 47%	Age group: 20–29 29% 30–39 49% >40 22% male 38% female 62% Occupation: CEO 28%; Senior Manager 12%; Manager 9%; Professional 14%

Best Life Shangri-la	New Wealthy Lifestyle	2007	Infotown Group	First-/Second-/Third-Tier Cities	100,000	Private chamber/club 1.7%; Real estate 4.3%; Restaurant 5.5%; Spa/beauty parlor 5.5%; Hotel 46.1%; Golf club 1.9%; Luxury goods store 23.0%; Luxury car dealers 2.3%; Finance industry 2.1%; Airport 3.3%; Other 4.3% / Government 3%; Media/TV station 6%; Full-time wife 26%; Other 2% / Family incomes (monthly): <20,000 (US$2,941) 2%; 20,000–39,000 (US$2,941–5,735) 13%; 40,000–59,000 (US$5,882–8,677) 15%; 60,000–79,000 (US$8,823–11,618) 10%; 80,000–99,000 (US$11,765–14,559) 17%; >100,000 (US$14,706) 43%
Modern Weekly	Lifestyle Weekly		Modern Media Group	First-/Second-Tier Cities	497,500	Airport/hotel/subway 15%; Newsstand 50%; Supermarket 22%; Bookstore 13% / Age group: 18–24 12.2%; 25–34 69.4%; 35–45 18.4% / Education: Matriculation 25.6%; Bachelor's 56.9%; Master's or above 14.6%

(Continued)

Field	Arrival in China	Publisher	Chinese Partner	Coverage	Circulation	Distribution	Readership
							Other 2.9%
							<u>Type of enterprise</u>
							Government-owned 7%;
							Foreign-owned 16%;
							Sino-foreign joint venture 34%;
							Private 37%;
							Government sector 3%;
							Others 3%
							<u>Family income (RMB)</u>:
							<6,000 (US$882) 27.1%;
							6,000–10,000
							(US$882–1,471) 37.1%;
							10,000–14,000
							(US$1,471–2,059) 14.3%;
							14,000–20,000
							(US$2,059–2,941) 8%;
							20,000–30,000
							(US$2,941–4,412) 7.1%;
							>30,000 (US$4,412) 3.5%;
							Other 3%

*US$ figures based on February 2008 exchange rate of RMB6.8 = US$1.

National Television Audience Ratings (as at 24 September 2008)

Channel	Whole Day (per 1,000 viewers)	Channel	18:00–24:00 (per 1,000 viewers)
CCTV1	0.84	CCTV1	2.02
CCTV3	0.52	CCTV5	1.02
CCTV5	0.46	CCTV3	1
CCTV6	0.44	CCTV8	0.94
CCTV8	0.42	CCTV6	0.76
Hunan TV	0.34	CCTV4	0.61
CCTV4	0.3	Hunan TV	0.6
CCTV2	0.29	CCTV2	0.59
CCTV News	0.27	CCTV News	0.48
Jiangsu TV	0.2	Jiangsu TV	0.45
CCTV kids	0.18	CCTV Kids	0.37
Anhui TV	0.17	Chongqing TV	0.3
CCTV 10	0.17	CCTV10	0.3
Chongqing TV	0.16	Zhejiang TV	0.28
Zhejiang TV	0.15	Beijing TV	0.28
Sichuan TV	0.15	Tianjing TV	0.28
Tianjin TV	0.14	Anhui TV	0.25
Shandong TV	0.13	Shandong TV	0.25
BTV	0.13	CCTV7	0.25
Dragon TV	0.12	Dragon TV	0.24

(Continued)

Channel	Whole Day (per 1,000 viewers)	Channel	18:00–24:00 (per 1,000 viewers)
Jiangxi TV	0.12	Sichuan TV	0.24
CCTV7	0.12	CCTV12	0.23
CCTV12	0.11	Heilongjiang TV	0.22
Heilongjiang TV	0.1	Jiangxi TV	0.2
Liaoning TV	0.1	Henan TV	0.18
Henan TV	0.08	Liaoning TV	0.18
Yunnan TV	0.07	CCTV11	0.13
Guangxi TV	0.07	Yunnan TV	0.12
Jilin TV	0.07	Hebei TV	0.12
CCTV11	0.07	Guangxi TV	0.11
Hubei TV	0.06	Hubei TV	0.1
Hebei TV	0.06	Jilin TV	0.1
Guangdong TV	0.05	Guangdong TV	0.09
Guizhou TV	0.04	Fujian TV	0.09
Fujian TV	0.04	Guizhou TV	0.08
Inner Mongolia TV	0.03	Tourism TV	0.07
Shanxi TV	0.03	Inner Mongolia TV	0.06
Tourism TV	0.03	Shanxi TV	0.06
Qinghai TV	0.02	Shaanxi TV	0.04
Shaanxi TV	0.02	CCTV Music	0.04
CCTV Music	0.02	Qinghai TV	0.03
Ningxia TV	0.01	CCTV9	0.03
Gansu TV	0.01	Ningxia TV	0.02
CCTV9	0.01	Gansu TV	0.02
Tibet TV	0	Tibet TV	0

Source: ACNielsen

Brands with Approved Well-Known Trademark Status

	Trademark in Chinese	Trademark
1	吉列	Gillette
2	迪士尼	Disney
3	麦当劳及 M 图	McDonald's
4	M 图	Motorola
5	杜邦	Dupont
6	绿箭	Doublemint
7	美标	American Standard
8	帝舵表及图*	Tudor
9	美洲虎图形*	Jaguar
10	兰蔻*	Lancôme
11	BOSS*	Boss
12	法拉利*	Ferrari
13	金利来及图*	Goldlion
14	飞利浦及图	Philips

(Continued)

*As at the end of 2008, this denotes international luxury brand.

	Trademark in Chinese	Trademark
15	浩沙 HAOSHA	HOSA
16	F1 FORMULA1	Formula 1
17	卡地亚*	Cartier
18	天梭*	Tissot
19	正新及图	CST
20	梦特娇*	Montagut
21	西瓜太郎及图	Melon Boy
22	周大福*	Chow Tai Fook
23	NISSAN 尼桑	Nissan
24	YKK	YKK
25	DE BEERS 戴比尔斯*	De Beers
26	YSL YVES SAINT LAURENT*	Yves Saint Laurent
27	香格里拉 SHANGRI-LA*	Shangri-La
28	周大生 CHOW TAI SENG*	Chow Tai Seng
29	百丽 BELLE	Belle
30	德芙	Dove
31	米其林 MICHELIN 及图	Michelin
32	大金 DAIKIN 及图	Daikin
33	埃索 ESSO 及图	Esso
34	斯得雅	Stava
35	舒肤佳	Safeguard
36	柯达	Kodak
37	SΛMSUNG	Samsung
38	欧莱雅 L'OREAL*	L'oreal
39	上好佳 及图形	Oishi
40	NESCAFE	Nescafe
41	哈森 HARSON 及图	Harson
42	李锦记 LEE KUM KEE 及图	Lee Kum Kee
43	Panasonic	Panasonic
44	HONDA	Honda
45	丰田*	Toyota
46	PORSCHE 保时捷*	Porsche
47	红牛 RedBull 及图	RedBull
48	统一	P Unif
49	哥弟 GIRDEAR	Girdear

	Trademark in Chinese	Trademark
50	震旦	Aurora
51	侨鑫 KINGOLD	Kingold
52	金至尊 及图	3d-gold
53	GOOGLE	Google
54	BENQ	BENQ
55	雅培	Abbott Laboratories
56	雅芳 AVON*	Avon
57	STARBUCKS 及图	Starbucks
58	KAWASAKI 及图	Kawasaki
69	爱普生 EPSON	Epson
60	LEXUS 及图	Lexus
61	PRUDENTIAL	Prudential
62	PIRELLI	Pirelli
63	爱得利 IVORY	Ivory
64	乐力 OSTEOFORM	Osteoform
65	PORTS INTERNATIONAL/寳姿	Ports
66	PIONEER/ 先锋	Pioneer
67	金龙鱼 ARAWANA 及图	Arawana
68	戴尔	Dell
69	NOKIA 诺基亚	Nokia
70	NCR	NCR
71	宏碁 ACER	Acer
72	米盖尔 及图	Miquel
73	SUN	Sun
74	嘉实多	Castrol
75	BP 及图	BP
76	SANYO	Sanyo
77	诗芬	Sifone
78	好丽友	Orion
79	ORLANE*	Orlane
80	罗技	Logitech
81	班尼路 BALENO	Baleno
82	高露洁	Colgate
83	爱登堡	Edenbo

(Continued)

	Trademark in Chinese	Trademark
84	双立人 及图形	Sigmabond
85	百度	Baidu
86	美宝莲 Maybelline*	Maybelline
87	自然美 NATURAL BEAUTY*	Natural Beauty
88	竹盐	Bamboo Salt
89	群豪 Qunhao 及图	Qun Hao
90	绅浪	Sunland
91	老爷车 LAO YE CHE 及图	Lao Ye Che
92	旺旺	want want
93	PENTIUM	Pentium
94	東芝	Toshiba
95	图形	Uthai
96	劳力士	Rolex
97	沃尔玛	Wal-Mart
98	霍尼韦尔	Honeywell
99	立邦	Nippon Paint
100	永和 及图形	Yon Ho
101	舒肤佳	Safeguard
102	亨奈威尔	Honywell

Source: Wanhuida Law Firm Beijing, 2008

Barthe, Roland. *Le système de la mode*. Seuil, 1983.

Bastien, Vincent and Kapferer, Jean Noël. *The luxury strategy: Break the rules of marketing to build luxury brands*. Kogan papers, 2008.

Belk, R. W. "Materialism: Trait Aspects of Living in the Material World," *Journal of Consumer Research* 12 (3) 1985.

Blanckaert, Christian. *Luxe*. Le Cherche Midi, 2007.

Bosoian, Michael and de Poix, Alix. *India by design: The pursuit of luxury and Fashion*. John Wiley and Sons, 2009.

Castarede, Jean. *Le Luxe, Que sais-je?* (5th edition) PUF, 2008.

Castarede, Jean and Rouart, Jean Marie. *Luxe et civilisation: Histoire mondiale*. Eyrolles, 2008.

Chada, Radha and Husband, Paul. *The cult of luxury brand: Inside Asia's love affair with luxury*. Nicholas Brealey International, 2006.

Chevalier, Michel and Mazzalovo, Gérald. *Luxury Brand Management: A World of Privilege*. John Wiley & Sons (Asia) Pte. Ltd., 2008.

Chevalier, Michel and Mazzalovo, Gérald, *Pro Logo*. Palgrave Macmillan, 2004.

Cole, L. and Sherrell, D. "Comparing Scales to Measure Compulsive Buying: An Exploration of Their Dimensionality," *Advances in Consumer Research* 22 (1) 1995.

Cosmetic News, China, September 2007, overseas issue No.46 (1).

Cui, G. and Liu, Q. "Executive Insights: Emerging Market Segments in a Transitional Economy: A study of Urban Consumers in China," *Journal of International Marketing* 9 (1), 2001.

Danziger, Pamela. *Let them eat cake. Marketing luxury to the masses as well as the classes*. Kaplan Business, 2005.

Deng Xiaoping, "Seize the opportunity to develop the economy," in *Selected works of Deng Xiaoping Volume* 3. Beijing, 1979.

Doctoroff, Tom. *Billions, selling to the new Chinese consumer*. Palgrave Macmillan, 2005.

Dubois, B., Laurent, G. and Czellar, S. 2000, "*Consumer Rapport to Luxury: Analyzing Complex and Ambivalent Attitudes*," Working paper HEC.

Epstein, S. "Cognitive-experiential self-theory" in L. Pervin (ed.). *Handbook of Personality: Theory and Research*. The Guilford Press, 1990.

Epstein, S., Pacini, R. and Denes, R. V. "Individual differences in intuitive-experiential and analytical-rational thinking styles," *Journal of Personality and Social Psychology* 71 (2) 1996.

Faber, R. and O'Guinn, T. "A Clinical Screener for Compulsive Buying," *Journal of Consumer Research*, 1992.

Far Eastern Economic Review 2002, "China's Elite Report," Hong Kong.

Frank, Robert H. *Luxury Fever*. Princeton University Press, 1999.

Gutman, J. "A Means-Ends Chain model based on consumer categorization processes," *Journal of Marketing* 46 (1) 1982.

Hofstede, Geert. *Cultures and organizations: Software of the mind: Intercultural cooperation and its importance for survival*. New York: McGraw-Hill, 1991.

Hsu, F.L.K. *American and Chinese: Passages to Differences*. Honolulu: University of Howaii Press, 1981.

Jacoberger-Lavoué, V. "Comité Colbert: Objectif Chine" in *Valeurs Actuelles*, 20 November 2008.

Kotler, Philip, *Marketing Management* (10th edition). Prentice Hall: 1996.

KPMG 2007, "China's luxury consumers: Moving up the curve."

KPMG–TNS 2008, "China's Luxury Consumers, moving up the curve."

Laurent, Gilles, "Luxury for the happy many" in *Marketing for the global business*. FT Putman Publishing, 1998.

"Le marché de luxe en Chine et à Hong Kong," *UBIFRANCE*: March 2007.

Le Nagard-Assayag, Emmanuelle and Pras, Bernard. "Innovation et marketing stratégique" in P. Muster and H. Penan (eds) *Encyclopédie de l'innovation*, Paris: Economica, 2003.

"Lifestyle report for Chinese affluent households," China Economic Monitoring and Analysis Center, June 2007.

"Luxury products struggle for profit in China," Le Hin Lim, *International Herald Tribune*, February 1, 2007.

Mastercard/HSBC joint study on China Affluent, 2007.

McCracken, Grant. "Who is the Celebrity Endorser? Cultural Foundations of the Endorsement Process," *Journal of Consumer Research*, 1989.

Michman, Ronald D. and Maze, Ewald M. *The affluent consumer: Marketing and selling the luxury lifestyle*. Praeger Publishers, 2006.

Netemeyer, G., Burton, S. and Lichtenstein, D. R. "Trait aspects of vanity: measurement and relevance to consumer behavior," *Journal of Consumer Research* 21 (4) 1995.

Nisbett, R. E., Peng, K. P., Choi, I. and Norenzayan, A. "Culture and system of Thought: Holistic Versus Analytic Cognition," *Psychological Review* 108 (2) 2001.

Oechsli, Matt. *The Art of Selling the Affluent: How to Attract, Service and Retain the Wealthy Consumers and Clients for Life*. John Wiley & Sons, 2004.

Okonkwo, Uche. *Luxury on line*. Palgrave Macmillan, 2008.

Ordish, Rebecca and Adcock, Alan. *China Intellectual Property Challenges and Solutions*. John Wiley & Sons, 2008.

Rogers, Everett M. *Diffusion of Innovations*. Free Press Glencoe, 1962.

Rokeach, Milton. *The Nature of Human Values*. Free Press, 1973.

Schiffman, Leon and Kanuk, Leslie. *Consumer Behavior* (7th Edition). Prentice Hall, Inc. and Tsinghua University Press, 2000.

Schütte, Hellmut and Ciarlante, Deanne. *Consumer Behavior in Asia*. MacMillan Business, 1998.

Silverstein, Michael and Fiske, Niel. *Trading up: The new American luxury*. Portfolio Hardcover, 2003.

Thomas, Dana. *Deluxe, how luxury lost its luster*. Penguin Books, 2007.

Tsai, Jacqueline. *La Chine et le Luxe*. Odile Jacob, 2008.

Twitchell, James. *Living it up: Our Love Affair with Luxury*. Columbia University Press, 2002.

Vaughn, Richard. "How Advertising Works: A Planning Model," *Journal of Advertising Research* 20 (5): (1980).

Veblen, Thorstein. *The Theory of the Leisure Class*. MacMillan, 1899.

Vertumne International & Associés, "The Chinese wine market: Opportunities and Threats."

Wong, N. and Ahuvia, A. "Personal Taste and Family Face: Luxury Consumption in Confucian and Western Societies," *Psychology and Marketing* 15 (5): 1997.

Xiao Lu, Pierre. *Elite China, Luxury Consumer Behavior in China*. John Wiley & Sons, 2008.

Zhang Fengming, "Young drive spending on luxuries," *Shanghai Daily*, November 30, 2006.